B LOOM'S

ReViews

COMPREHENSIVE RESEARCH & STUDY GUIDES

William Shakespeare's

King Lear

Edited & with
an Introduction
by Harold Bloom

Printed and bound in the United States of America.

The Chelsea House World Wide Web site address is
http://www.chelseahouse.com

First Printing
1 3 5 7 9 8 6 4 2

Library of Congress Cataloging-in-Publication Data

William Shakespeare's King Lear / edited and with an introduction by Harold Bloom.
p   cm.—(Bloom's Notes)
Includes bibliographical references and index.
Summary: Includes a brief biography of the author, thematic and structural analysis of the work, critical views, and an index of themes and ideas.
ISBN 0-7910-4065-8 (hc)   0-7910-4134-4 (pb)
1. Shakespeare, William, 1564-1616. King Lear. 2. Lear, King (Legendary character), in literature. 3. Tragedy. [1. Shakespeare, William, 1564-1616. King Lear. 2. English literature--History and criticism.]
I. Bloom, Harold. II. Series.
PR2819.W54   1995
822.3'3—dc20
95-45103
CIP
AC

Chelsea House Publishers
1974 Sproul Road, Suite 400
P.O. Box 914
Broomall, PA 19008-0914

Contents

Editor's Note   4

Introduction   5

Biography of William Shakespeare   8

Thematic and Structural Analysis   13

List of Characters   27

Critical Views
    Samuel Johnson on the Moral Issues in the Play   29
    Samuel Taylor Coleridge on Edmund   31
    A. C. Bradley on the Pessimism of the Play   33
    Leo Tolstoy on the Failings of the Play   35
    Lily B. Campbell on the Vanity of King Lear   37
    George Orwell on Tolstoy, Lear, and Renunciation   39
    Robert Bechtold Heilman on Age in the Play   41
    Irving Ribner on Regeneration in the Play   44
    John Holloway on Evil in the Play   46
    Josephine Waters Bennett on Lear's Madness   48
    William Rosen on Lear and the Nature of Kingship   52
    Northrop Frye on Tragedy and Melodrama   54
    Roy W. Battenhouse on Lear's "Darker Purpose"   55
    Frank Kermode on Delusions and Reality in the Play   57
    Ruth Nevo on the Importance of Love in the Play   58
    Bernard McElroy on the Nature of Monarch's Power   61
    Paul Delany on Feudalism and the Play   63
    William F. Zak on Cordelia   66
    C. L. Barber and Richard P. Wheeler on Lear's Second Childhood   69
    Alexander Leggatt on Staging the Play   72
    David M. Bergeron on Letters in the Play   75

Works by William Shakespeare   78

Works about William Shakespeare and *King Lear*   81

Index of Themes and Ideas   84

Editor's Note

My Introduction argues that an aspect of Lear is based upon the biblical Solomon, and that there are no limits to the sense in which Lear's tragedy remains a pre-Christian, rather than a Christian drama.

The copious Critical Views commence with Dr. Samuel Johnson's Christian revulsion to Cordelia's murder, and with Coleridge's brilliant portrait of the arch-villain Edmund. A. C. Bradley accurately sees the pervasiveness of the play's cosmological despair; so does the greatest of novelists, Tolstoy, but his Christian intensity causes him to reject the tragedy as an absurdity.

Lear's self-love is perhaps overstressed by Lily B. Campbell, while the novelist George Orwell defends the drama against Shakespeare by rather oddly seeing it as exalting renunciation as such. I find much more apt the subtle emphasis upon Lear's extreme old age by R. B. Heilman, who links destructiveness and learning as antithetical elements in the aging process. A more hopeful view is taken by Irving Ribner, who finds regeneration to be a dominant pattern in the play, a position somewhat nullified by John Holloway's analysis of evil in *King Lear.*

Lear's madness is shrewdly anatomized by Josephine Waters Bennett, while William Rosen centers instead upon the ways in which Lear is every inch a king. The great critic Northrop Frye vindicates the play's status as being beyond melodrama, after which a Christianizing reading is attempted by Roy W. Battenhouse, for whom Lear is almost wholly culpable. I prefer Frank Kermode's reminder that we must distinguish between "the two bodies of the king," and Ruth Nevo's defense of the purgative nature of Lear's sufferings.

Questions of monarchial power and control are examined by Bernard McElroy and Paul Delany, after which William F. Zak studies Cordelia's role as one that seems to depart from the frightening despair of the rest of the drama.

Lear's madness returns as central in the excerpt from C. L. Barber and Richard Wheeler, who regard the king as regressing into a world of second childhood. The technical difficulties of staging the apocalyptic storm scene engross Alexander Leggatt, after which David Bergeron chronicles the vital role that deadly letters take on in this darkest of all literary tragedies.

Introduction

HAROLD BLOOM

There are only a necessarily small number of literary works that impress us as having reached the limits of art, and some of them cause dispute when they are placed at that eminence. *The Tragedy of King Lear* has persuaded nearly everyone who has read it or seen it performed that nothing in language can go beyond it. Only Count Leo Tolstoy was an exception; he despised the play and raved against it, perhaps because it prophesied uncannily an end that largely became his own. More overtly, he denounced it for impiety and immorality; it certainly does offend you if you believe that God's justice somehow prevails in this world. Shakespeare, entering the least secular of all his dramas, carefully chose pre-Christian Britain as the place and time of this cosmological vision. The Christian audience beheld a legendary Celtic king, who worships pagan gods, but they were aware of the strangely biblical aura of this play. They were being shown an ancestral king, in Old Testament times, long before the coming of Christ. There are several echoes of the Book of Job in Lear's tragedy, but I do not think that Lear truly resembles Job. The biblical archetype for Lear is Solomon the Wise, who reigned for half a century over the Israelites and whose death was followed by the catastrophic breakup of his kingdom. Lear does not resemble Solomon in all his glory, as he appears in Kings, Chronicles, and the Song of Songs, but a very different Solomon, the old sage of Ecclesiastes, the Proverbs, and The Wisdom of Solomon, for us part of the Apocrypha but very much integrated into the Geneva Bible, which was the mature Shakespeare's text. Lear echoes this Solomon:

> I myself am also mortal and a man like all other, and am come of him that was first made of the earth. . . .
> And when I was borne, I received the commune aire, and fel upon the earth, which is of like nature, crying and weeping at the first as all other do. . . .
> For there is no King that had anie other beginning of birth. All men then have one entrance into life, and a like going out.
> (Geneva Bible, Wisdome of Salomon, VII: 1, 3, 5–6)

"Fools" in Shakespeare can mean "dear ones," "dupes," "idiots," "court jesters," or "victims," that is, objects of pity. "This great stage of fools" comprises all of these but "victims" in particular. Lear, like Solomon, though king, is man like all others and comes into the world crying and weeping, implicitly understanding that he too will go out in the same way. The great theatrical metaphor, "this great stage of fools," is Lear's judgment upon his own tragedy, and Shakespeare's vision of all tragedy. Neither Lear's judgment nor Shakespeare's vision, at least in the play, is reconcilable with a Christian view that Lear's suffering is redeemed or redeemable. In a T. S. Eliotic, neo-Christian reading like that of Maynard Mack, *The Tragedy of King Lear* resembles Samuel Taylor Coleridge's *The Rime of the Ancient Mariner,* and both Lear and the Mariner emerge from the waste land into the salvation of a sacramental universe. But Shakespeare, as I have remarked, took care to station this drama nine centuries before Christ, so that the legendary king of Britain, Lear, and the wise Solomon were near-contemporaries. The world of Ecclesiastes and Wisdom, like that of *King Lear,* is anything but a sacramental realm. The best study of the play's theology, William R. Elton's King Lear *and the Gods* (1966), reaches the conclusion that a Christian and therefore optimistic interpretation is invalid because "Lear is shown to develop from pagan belief to disbelief." Lear is not saved or redeemed, and no benign providence can accommodate the injustice of Cordelia's death. Elton sensibly compares *King Lear* to *Hamlet* as a skeptical work that leaves us with a highly deliberate "confusion of values." The play, according to Elton, has clear Christian allusions, but essentially is a "pagan tragedy." A Christian playgoer, and King James I in particular, could conclude that the necessity of the Christian revelation was implied by Shakespeare's drama, and a skeptical Jacobean intellectual could reach an opposite conclusion, one that questioned every possibility of faith.

If Ecclesiastes and the Wisdom of Solomon, rather than Job, served Shakespeare as models, then the central moment in *King Lear* comes in Edgar's remonstrance to his father, Gloucester, when the blind man refuses to go further and says, "a man may rot even here." There is authentic authority in Edgar's rejoinder:

> What! in ill thoughts again? Men must endure
> Their going hence, even as their coming hither:
> Ripeness is all. Come on.

Hamlet, speaking to Horatio about his imminent, climactic duel with Laertes, says that "The readiness is all," where "readiness" means "willing." Edgar confirms Lear's earlier echo of The Wisdom of Solomon, but also Ecclesiastes, chapter three, with its emphasis that to everything there is a season, an appropriate time that cannot be denied. The season at the close of *King Lear* is past harvest, the time is very late, and Edgar concludes the drama with a couplet that is the essence of belatedness:

> The oldest hath borne most: we that are young
> Shall never see so much, nor live so long. ✤

Biography of William Shakespeare

Few events in the life of William Shakespeare are supported by reliable evidence, and many incidents recorded by commentators of the last four centuries are either conjectural or apocryphal.

William Shakespeare was born in Stratford-upon-Avon on April 22 or 23, 1564, the son of Mary Arden and John Shakespeare, a tradesman. His very early education was in the hands of a tutor, for his parents were probably illiterate. At age seven he entered the Free School in Stratford, where he learned the "small Latin and less Greek" attributed to him by Ben Jonson. When not in school Shakespeare may have gone to the popular Stratford fairs and to the dramas and mystery plays performed by traveling actors.

When Shakespeare was about thirteen his father removed him from school and apprenticed him to a butcher, although it is not known how long he remained in this occupation. When he was eighteen he married Anne Hathaway; their first child, Susanna, was born six months later. A pair of twins, Hamnet and Judith, were born in February 1585. About this time Shakespeare was caught poaching deer on the estate of Sir Thomas Lucy of Charlecot; Lucy's prosecution is said to have inspired Shakespeare to write his earliest literary work, a satire on his opponent. Shakespeare was convicted of poaching and forced to leave Stratford. He withdrew to London, leaving his family behind. He soon attached himself to the stage, initially in a menial capacity (as tender of playgoers' horses, according to one tradition), then as prompter's attendant. When the poaching furor subsided, Shakespeare returned to Stratford to join one of the many bands of itinerant actors. In the next five years he gained what little theater training he received.

By 1592 Shakespeare was a recognized actor, and in that year he wrote and produced his first play, *Henry VI, Part One*. Its success impelled Shakespeare soon afterward to write the second and third parts of *Henry VI*. (Many early and modern critics believed that *Love's Labour's Lost* preceded these histories as Shakespeare's earliest play, but the majority of modern scholars discount this theory.) Shakespeare's popularity provoked the jealousy of Robert Greene, as recorded in his posthumous *Groats-worth of Wit* (1592).

In 1593 Shakespeare published *Venus and Adonis,* a long poem based upon Ovid (or perhaps upon Arthur Golding's translation of Ovid's *Metamorphoses*). It was dedicated to the young earl of Southampton—but perhaps without permission, a possible indication that Shakespeare was trying to gain the nobleman's patronage. However, the dedicatory address to Southampton in the poem *The Rape of Lucrece* (1594) reveals Shakespeare to have been on good terms with him. Many plays—such as *Titus Andronicus, The Comedy of Errors,* and *Romeo and Juliet*—were produced over the next several years, most performed by Shakespeare's troupe, the Lord Chamberlain's Company. In December 1594 Shakespeare acted in a comedy (of unknown authorship) before Queen Elizabeth; many other royal performances followed in the next decade.

In August 1596 Shakespeare's son Hamnet died—a loss that may have been seminal to the writing of *Hamlet* approximately five years later. Early the next year Shakespeare bought a home, New Place, in the center of Stratford; he is said to have planted a mulberry tree in the backyard with his own hands. Shakespeare's relative prosperity is indicated by his purchase of more than a hundred acres of farmland in 1602, a cottage near his estate later that year, and half-interest in the tithes of some local villages in 1605.

In September 1598 Shakespeare began his friendship with the then unknown Ben Jonson by producing his play *Every Man in His Humour.* The next year the publisher William Jaggard affixed Shakespeare's name, without his permission, to a curious medley of poems under the title *The Passionate Pilgrim;* the majority of the poems were not by Shakespeare. Two of his sonnets, however, appeared in this collection, although the 154 sonnets, with their mysterious dedication to "Mr. W. H.," were not published as a group until 1609. Also in 1599 the Globe Theatre was built in Southwark (an area of London), and Shakespeare's company began acting there. Many of his greatest plays—*Troilus and Cressida, King Lear, Othello, Macbeth*—were performed in the Globe before its destruction by fire in 1613.

The death in 1603 of Queen Elizabeth, the last of the Tudors, and the accession of James I, from the Stuart dynasty of Scotland, created anxiety throughout England. Shakespeare's fortunes, however, were unaffected, as the new monarch extended the license of Shakespeare's company to perform at the Globe. James I saw a performance of *Othello* at the court in November 1604. In October 1605 Shakespeare's company performed before the Mayor and Corporation of Oxford.

The last five years of Shakespeare's life seem void of incident; he had retired from the stage by 1613. Among the few known incidents is Shakespeare's involvement in a heated and lengthy dispute about the enclosure of common-fields around Stratford. He died on April 23, 1616, and was buried in the Church of St. Mary's in Stratford. A monument to him was later erected in the Poets' Corner of Westminster Abbey.

Numerous corrupt quarto editions of Shakespeare's plays were published during his lifetime. These editions, based on either manuscripts, promptbooks, or sometimes merely actors' recollections of the plays, were meant to capitalize on Shakespeare's renown. Other plays, now deemed wholly or largely spurious—*Edward III, The Yorkshire Tragedy* and others—were also published under Shakespeare's name during and after his lifetime. Shakespeare's plays were collected in the First Folio of 1623 by John Heminge and Henry Condell. Nine years later the Second Folio was published, and in 1640 Shakespeare's poems were collected. The first standard collected edition was by Nicholas Rowe (1709), followed by the editions of Alexander Pope (1723–1725), Lewis Theobald (1733), Samuel Johnson (1765), Edmond Malone (1790), and many others.

Shakespeare's plays are now customarily divided into the following categories (probable dates of writing are given in brackets): comedies (*The Comedy of Errors* [1590], *The Taming of the Shrew* [1592], *The Two Gentlemen of Verona* [1592–93], *A Midsummer Night's Dream* [1595], *Love's Labour's Lost*

[1595], *The Merchant of Venice* [1596–98], *As You Like It* [1597], *The Merry Wives of Windsor* [1597], *Much Ado About Nothing* [1598–99], *Twelfth Night* [1601], *All's Well That Ends Well* [1603–04], and *Measure for Measure* [1604]); histories (*Henry VI, Part One* [1590–92], *Henry VI, Parts Two and Three* [1590–92], *Richard III* [1591], *King John* [1591–98], *Richard II* [1595], *Henry IV, Part One* [1597], *Henry IV, Part Two* [1597], *Henry V* [1599], and *Henry VIII* [1613]); tragedies (*Titus Andronicus* [1590], *Romeo and Juliet* [1595], *Julius Caesar* [1599], *Hamlet* [1599–1601], *Troilus and Cressida* [1602], *Othello* [1602–04], *King Lear* [1604–05], *Macbeth* [1606], *Timon of Athens* [1607], *Antony and Cleopatra* [1606–07], and *Coriolanus* [1608]); romances (*Pericles, Prince of Tyre* [1606–08], *Cymbeline* [1609–10], *The Winter's Tale* [1610–11], and *The Tempest* [1611]). However, Shakespeare defied the canons of classical drama by mingling comedy, tragedy, and history, so that in some cases classification is debatable or arbitrary.

Shakespeare's reputation, while subject to many fluctuations, was firmly established by the eighteenth century. Samuel Johnson remarked, "Perhaps it would not be easy to find any authour, except Homer, who invented so much as Shakespeare, who so much advanced the studies which he cultivated, who effused so much novelty upon his age or country. The form, the characters, the language, and the shows of the English drama are his." Early in the nineteenth century Samuel Taylor Coleridge declared, "The Englishman who without reverence, a proud and affectionate reverence, can utter the name of William Shakespeare, stands disqualified for the office of critic. . . . Great as was the genius of Shakespeare, his judgment was at least equal to it."

A curious controversy developed in the middle of the nineteenth century in regard to the authorship of Shakespeare's plays, some contending that Sir Francis Bacon was the actual author of the plays, others (including Mark Twain) advancing the claims of the earl of Oxford. None of these attempts has succeeded in persuading the majority of scholars that Shakespeare himself is not the author of the plays attributed to him.

In recent years many landmark editions of Shakespeare, with increasingly accurate texts and astute critical commentary, have emerged. These include the *Arden Shakespeare* (1951) the *Oxford Shakespeare* (1982), and the *New Cambridge Shakespeare* (1984). Such critics as T. S. Eliot, G. Wilson Knight, Northrop Frye, W. H. Auden, and many others have continued to elucidate Shakespeare, his work, and his times, and he remains the most written-about author in the history of English literature. ❖

Thematic and Structural Analysis

Shakespeare's tragedy *King Lear,* written in 1605 or 1606, is set in pre-Christian Britain. The play opens in King Lear's palace, where the earls of Kent and Gloucester, and Edmund, the son of Gloucester, await the arrival of the king while discussing the impending partition of the kingdom (**Act I, scene 1**). We learn that Gloucester has two sons: Edmund, his beloved illegitimate child, and an older legitimate son, his heir. King Lear enters, followed by his daughters Goneril and Regan; their husbands, the dukes of Albany and Cornwall; his daughter Cordelia; and attendants. The king announces his decision to "shake cares and business from our age" by dividing his kingdom among his daughters and ceding his power to them and their husbands. The size of each daughter's allotment will depend upon her answer to his question: "Which of you shall we say doth love us most."

Goneril and Regan extravagantly profess their love and receive ample lands. However, Cordelia, the youngest and best-loved daughter, cannot answer the question. When asked to reply, she says, "I love your Majesty according to my bond, no more nor less." Stung by her apparent callousness, Lear furiously disowns her: "Here I disclaim all my paternal care, / Propinquity and property of blood. / And as a stranger to my heart and me / Hold thee from this for ever." The king divides Cordelia's share of the kingdom between her sisters and announces that henceforth he and his retinue of one hundred knights will divide their time month by month between the homes of Goneril and Regan.

The earl of Kent, a loyal follower of Lear who loves him as a father, protests the "hideous rashness" of this treatment of Cordelia; he hints that Lear is mad and states that Cordelia's words do not mean that she is unloving, but rather that she cannot grossly flatter. "Out of my sight!" exclaims Lear, banishing him. Kent's rebuke "See better, Lear," establishes one of the play's central themes: A lack of insight and an inability to see the truth result in misguided judgments and, eventually, tragedy.

13

Cordelia, courted by two suitors, is now disinherited and banished. The duke of Burgundy spurns her, but the king of France, recognizing Cordelia's strength of character, deems her "most rich being poor" and claims her as his queen. Cordelia says good-bye to her sisters and bids them take care of Lear, wishing, however, that he could be elsewhere because she recognizes her sisters' deceitfulness. By the close of the first scene, Shakespeare has established a central conflict in the play: the clash between the loyal and obedient characters and the treacherous, grasping ones. He shows Lear to be proud, hasty, peremptory, and misguided.

Act I, scene 2 takes place in the earl of Gloucester's castle. Edmund reveals his base nature in an opening soliloquy. He schemes to trick his father to gain control of the land of his brother Edgar, Gloucester's heir. Edmund presents Gloucester with a letter, purported to be written by Edgar, that asks Edmund to conspire against their father to gain control of his power and wealth. Gloucester reads it and is immediately enraged, calling Edgar an "unnatural, detested, brutish villain." The treacherous Edmund offers to talk with Edgar to learn his intentions. However, when he speaks with the innocent Edgar, he warns him that he has offended their father and suggests that he arm himself.

This subplot is a variation on the main plot. Both demarcate the "good" children from the "bad" children and pit the dutiful against the faithless, and children against their fathers. In each, the natural world serves as a mirror, reflecting the tension between the virtuous and the treacherous. To Gloucester, the unnatural late eclipses of the sun and moon portend no good:

> This villain of mine comes under the prediction, there's son against father; the King falls from the bias of nature, there's father against child. We have seen the best of our time: machinations, hollowness, treachery, and all ruinous disorders, follow us disquietly to our graves.

The confusion that Lear feels in scene 1 at Cordelia's seeming rejection also signals a violation of natural order. Cordelia has thrown his world into confusion with her transgression of the laws that govern parent-child relations.

However, both Gloucester and Lear misplace their blame. Gloucester does not realize that the actions the eclipse predicts are those of Edmund, not Edgar. Lear does not understand that Cordelia's assertion that she loves him "according to my bond, no more nor less" reflects a filial love that is natural, not the exaggerated love her sisters profess.

Act I, scene 3 occurs at the duke of Albany's palace, where Goneril and Oswald, her steward, discuss Lear's increasingly difficult behavior and the disorderly conduct of his knights. Goneril scorns her father for giving away his power and asserts that if he chafes at the restraints she plans to impose upon him and his retinue, then he can go early to Regan. This scene introduces Oswald as Goneril's supporter, equally contemptuous of the king.

In **Act I, scene 4**, a disguised Kent, still faithful to the king, offers his services to Lear. Lear discovers how poorly regarded he is by everyone in Albany's palace. Already upset, he is further angered by Oswald's insolence and strikes him. Kent trips Oswald and pushes him about, thus offering his first service to Lear and winning his affection. Lear's fool, who has been pining since Cordelia's departure, now gives his evaluation. He offers his fool's cap to Kent for taking the part of one out of favor. "Why this fellow has banished two on's daughters, and did the third a blessing against his will. If thou follow him, thou must needs wear my coxcomb." The fool can see that Lear has senselessly given his older daughters the means to strip him of everything. Throughout the play, the fool's words provide a biting commentary on the other characters' actions and hint at events to come. As Regan utters at the end of the play, "Jesters do oft prove prophets."

Goneril now informs Lear that the behavior of his insolent retinue is intolerable and tells him to reduce the number of his knights. Astounded that a daughter should so reprimand a father, Lear asks himself, "Where are his eyes?" Can a thing as unnatural as this disobedience be happening to him? Unable to stand this treatment any longer, he decides to leave at once for Regan's. He is beginning to recognize his blindness: Cordelia's fault was small, while his reaction to it was extreme and wrong-headed. Before leaving he calls upon nature to curse Goneril with barrenness or a child who is a "disnatured torment to her . . . that she may feel / How sharper than a serpent's tooth it is / To have a thankless child."

Goneril entrusts Oswald with a letter to Regan that documents their father's behavior and the imminent arrival of Lear and his retinue at Cornwall's castle. She anticipates Regan's support in further stripping Lear of any kingly power. Albany, however, mildly protests and thus begins to align himself against the treachery of his wife.

In the brief closing scene of Act I in the courtyard of Albany's palace, Lear, as he prepares to leave, gives Kent letters to take to Regan, who, he believes, loves him and will treat him kindly. The fool belittles his naïveté; Regan will behave just as Goneril has. Lear intimates that he has mistreated Cordelia and is tormented by thoughts of his own madness.

The whole of **Act II** takes place either in or just outside the earl of Gloucester's castle. In the **first scene**, Edmund and a courtier of Gloucester discuss the arrival that night of the duke of Cornwall and of Regan and the rumors of dissension between Cornwall and Albany. Cunning Edmund sees that he can use this information to further his scheme of turning his father against his brother. He calls Edgar from his hiding place and advises him to flee for his life because he is believed to have spoken against the duke of Cornwall. While urging Edgar to escape, Edmund draws his sword to pretend to stop him. To lend veracity to his charade, Edmund wounds his own arm and cries out to his father. The scene convinces Gloucester that Edmund is a loyal and dutiful son, while Edgar is a villain to be hunted.

Cornwall and Regan arrive to find a heartsick Gloucester. Regan suggests that Edgar has been influenced by Lear's riotous knights. Cornwall praises Edmund for his virtue and obedience, welcoming him as a loyal follower. He and Regan, having received letters from both Goneril and Lear about the pair's conflicts, have come to Gloucester to receive advice and to avoid encountering Lear at their home.

In **scene 2**, Oswald and Kent, the emissaries of Goneril and Lear's letters, come to blows. We see the still-disguised Kent assaulting the foppish, cowardly Oswald. Edmund enters with rapier drawn (continuing his show of defender of virtue), followed by Cornwall, Regan, Gloucester, and servants. Kent bluntly denounces Oswald as a dishonest troublemaker, while Oswald claims that he has been unjustly insulted. The incensed Cornwall orders Kent to be put in the stocks. Gloucester, still loyal to the king, beseeches Cornwall not to impose such a degrading punishment upon Lear's messenger. Gloucester, deeply troubled by this monstrous insolence toward the king, acknowledges his sorrow to Kent but leaves him in his "shameful lodging." Kent reads a letter from Cordelia, who has been told of his disguising himself and of Lear's reversals, and then he sleeps.

In **Act II, scene 3**, Edgar emerges from a hollow tree in which he has been hiding. To avoid capture, he decides to disguise himself as an insane beggar. His resolution to endure "the winds and persecutions of the sky" and to abandon his true self foreshadows what will soon happen to Lear.

Lear arrives at Gloucester's castle with his fool and an attendant (**II.4**). He is bewildered by Regan and Cornwall's absence from their home. From the stocks, Kent calls to him. Lear cannot believe that Cornwall and Regan have put his messenger there and demands to know what happened. Angry at the absence of the respect he deserves both as a king and as a father, Lear enters the castle to find Regan. When he learns that Cornwall and Regan are too tired to see him, his anger turns to rage and confusion. The world is topsy-turvy: A king and father should command while a daughter must obey. That they do not wish to speak with him is intolerable. They must be roused.

After Regan and Cornwall appear and Kent is set free, the conversation begins with a semblance of cordiality. Lear recounts Goneril's cruelty, while Regan tries to persuade him that Goneril was treating him as an old man should be treated and that he should return to her. Lear protests, cursing Goneril, but when Regan says that he will soon despise her as well, he insists that Regan's kind nature would never provoke his wrath.

Regan, he says, "better know'st / The offices of nature, bond of childhood, / Effects of courtesy, dues of gratitude." Ironically, Lear uses the word bond, the term Cordelia used to describe her love.

As Lear begins to question who had put his man in the stocks, Oswald appears to herald Goneril's arrival. The presence of Goneril, Regan's warm welcome of her sister, and Cornwall's admission to setting Kent in the stocks all come as a series of blows to Lear. To his dismay, Lear finds that Regan does not want him to live with her unless he conforms to the strictures that both sisters now begin to impose. Struggling to maintain his sanity in the face of his daughters' vicious attacks, he exclaims, "I prithee, daughter, do not make me mad."

Lear refuses to return to Goneril (his words recall his banishment of Cordelia in Act I, scene 2). Yet he still calls Goneril his child: "But yet thou art my flesh, my blood, my daughter; / Or rather a disease that's in my flesh, / which I must call a mire. . . ." He turns to Regan, but she insists that she cannot take him and that when she does it will be with a maximum of twenty-five knights. As Goneril and Regan continue to jab at him, Lear's reason and emotions are battered. He will go to Goneril (forgetting that he has just said that he will see her no more) with fifty men. She counters by asking him why he even needs one man. After trying to maintain his composure and begging the heavens for patience, Lear calls his daughters "unnatural hags" upon whom he will wreak such revenge—he is unable to continue, so great is his distress. He leaves the castle, crying, "O fool, I shall go mad!"

Outside, a fierce storm begins to rage. No one expresses pity that Lear is out wandering in the tempest. Goneril even implies that he has brought his fate upon himself.

Act III, scene 1 is set amid the raging storm on an open heath. Kent and a gentleman discuss the wild ravings of the king, who is wandering through the storm, accompanied only by his fool. Kent imparts news of a division between Albany and Cornwall that is not yet widely known. The king of France, who has had secret agents in both dukes' houses, is about to invade England; in fact, some of France's soldiers have already landed. The gentleman should go at once to Dover to seek out Cordelia and give her news of her father.

In a famous scene (**III.2**), Lear rages wildly across the heath, assaulted by the storm's force but urging it on. He dares the storm to ". . . spit fire; spout rain. / Nor rain, wind, thunder, fire are my daughters." The storm mirrors what Lear in a future scene calls "the tempest in my mind." Further, it is a sign of the treachery that has beset England. Lear remarks that the gods have sent the storm to reveal and punish sinners.

Kent arrives and tries to persuade Lear to take shelter in a nearby hovel while he returns to Gloucester's castle to implore the stony-hearted inmates to open the doors and save them from the storm. Lear, with a new humbleness, shows concern for his fool, who utters a strange prophecy that concludes,

> When usurers tell their gold i'th'field;
> And bawds and whores do churches build—
> Then shall the realm of Albion
> Come to great confusion.
> Then comes the time, who lives to see't
> That going shall be us'd with feet.

In **Act III, scene 3** Gloucester shares with Edmund his distress at the way Cornwall and Regan, guests in his own castle, have turned against him because of his sympathy for Lear. Edmund appears to side with his father, who also confides that there is division between the dukes. Gloucester has a secret letter that tells of a powerful force forming to help the king. He will join it, even at risk of his life. Edmund must pretend everything is normal to Cornwall. Of course, deceitful Edmund will tell all because "[t]he younger rise when the old doth fall."

On the heath, Kent leads Lear to a hovel (**III.4**). Lear stays outside to pray. The storm in his mind and heart is so powerful that he can scarcely feel the "tyranny of the open night." However, he will try to endure; reflection on Regan and Goneril's "filial ingratitude" will only lead to madness. Lear's words also indicate a new-found compassion for the "[p]oor, naked, wretches," as he realizes that he has done little to better their conditions. By experiencing their misery, he hopes he will be able to help them, to bring them justice.

In the hovel, the fool discovers Edgar disguised as Tom, a crazed beggar barely covered by a ragged blanket. Lear can only believe that the beggar's madness and destitution are the results of unkind, treacherous daughters who have stripped him of all he ever had. Edgar, however, tells Lear that he was once a lustful and deceitful servant who has now fallen on misfortune. Lear feels kinship because he, too, has nothing left. To join Edgar in destitution, he begins to tear off his own clothes. When Gloucester, defying Cornwall and Regan, arrives with a torch to take Lear to a better shelter, he does not recognize his son and speaks sorrowfully to Kent (who is also still disguised) of the evil that he believes Edgar, whom he dearly loved, has done. He can feel madness claiming him just as it seems to have claimed Lear, who has meanwhile become entranced with mad Tom, calling him "noble philosopher" and insisting that he accompany them from the hovel.

Edmund betrays his father to Cornwall, who, having taken over Gloucester's castle, rewards him with the title of earl of Gloucester (**III.5**). Cornwall tells Edmund to find and apprehend his father, promising, "[T]hou shalt find a dearer father in my love."

Gloucester takes Lear, Kent, the fool, and Edgar to shelter in a farmhouse, and then leaves to find provisions (**III.6**). Lear's wits have now left him, and he proceeds to conduct a "trial" of his daughters with Edgar and the fool as judges. Poor Kent is deeply moved by this piteous sight and urges Lear to rest, but Lear is intent on justice, another issue that recurs throughout the play. Edgar is also moved to tears. Gloucester returns with urgent news that the king is hunted and must flee to Dover for protection. The scene closes with Edgar commenting that his own sorrow seems so much less in comparison with the misery of the king. He then prays for the king's safe escape.

Act III, scene 7 takes place in Gloucester's castle, where Cornwall presides over bustling activity. He dispatches Goneril and Edmund to Goneril's husband, Albany, with news about the landing of the French army—an enemy against whom the dukes must join forces—and sends his servants to seek the traitor Gloucester. Oswald arrives to report that Gloucester has managed to convey Lear and some of his knights to Dover.

Gloucester is then brought in and accused of treachery. Gloucester protests: Are not they his guests? At last he reveals his courage, stating that he has sided with the king because he could no longer stand their monstrous treatment of Lear: "I would not see thy cruel nails / Pluck out his poor old eyes." He declares, "I shall see / The winged vengeance overtake such children." Enraged, Cornwall gouges out one of his eyes and crushes it underfoot. A horrified servant vigorously protests, and Regan runs him through with a sword, but not before he severely wounds Cornwall, who still manages to gouge out Gloucester's remaining eye. Gloucester calls for Edmund to avenge this horrid act, but Regan triumphantly says that Edmund, far from loving his father, hates him and was the one who had informed against him. Gloucester, "seeing" at last his sons for what they truly are, cries, "Then Edgar was abused / Kind gods, forgive me that, and prosper him." He is thrust out of the castle to "smell" his way to Dover. Servants vow to follow him, put balm on his eyes, and find Tom the mad beggar to lead him.

Stoic Edgar, musing that to have experienced the worst is to know that change can only be for the better, encounters his father being led by an old man on the path from the castle (**IV.1**). He hears his father acknowledge the "blindness" of his earlier actions and cry out for his banished son. Edgar realizes that a situation he thought could become no worse just has. Gloucester tells the old man that during the previous night's storm he had seen a pitiful beggar, who had made him think "man a worm." He had thought also of Edgar, still believing him villainous. Now Gloucester knows differently and utters despairingly, "As flies to wanton boys are we to the gods— / They kill us for their sport."

Edgar realizes that he must not yet reveal himself. Gloucester dismisses his old retainer, asking him to get clothing for this beggar, who will lead him from now on. In his new wisdom and humility, he gives poor "Tom" his purse so that his wealth can be more justly distributed (like Lear, he is now concerned with justice) and asks to be led to Dover by way of a high cliff.

Outside Albany's palace (**IV.2**), Oswald warns Goneril, just arriving with Edmund, that Albany appears strangely changed.

He seems pleased at the landing of the French army, disgruntled at his wife's return, disdainful of Oswald, and sympathetic to Gloucester. Goneril, contemptuous of her husband, sends Edmund back to Cornwall to muster her brother-in-law's army against the French and declares that henceforth she will be in charge at home. She lustfully kisses Edmund before he leaves.

A newly forceful Albany enters; the two argue bitterly. To him, Goneril is "not worth the dust which the rude wind / Blows in your face." He recognizes her falsity and cruelty. Goneril, in turn, spurns Albany's manhood, calling him weak, "milk-livered," and a "moral fool." A messenger rushes in with news that Cornwall has died from a wound suffered during the earlier skirmish. To Albany, appalled at Gloucester's maiming, the news is proof of heavenly justice. He sees Edmund as a cruel opportunist and Gloucester as loyal to the king. Goneril, however, is concerned about Cornwall's death because it leaves Regan a widow and so a rival for Edmund's love.

Near Dover (**IV.3**), Kent learns that Cordelia received his letters with sadness and composure. She is horrified at her sisters' treatment of their father. Kent comments, "The stars above us, govern our conditions, / Else one self mate and make could not beget / Such different issues." Kent, still disguised, says that Lear is in Dover, but his actions toward Cordelia "sting his mind so venomously" that he is too ashamed to see her.

On a field near Dover (**IV.4**), Cordelia, her husband having been called back to France, enters with her soldiers and a doctor. She sends a soldier to find Lear, who is wandering nearby, "mad as the vexed sea." The doctor assures Cordelia there are natural medicinal plants that will give him rest and "close the eye of anguish." The British army approaches, but Cordelia is prepared to meet them, not simply to vanquish them, but to restore to her father what is rightly his.

In Gloucester's castle (**IV.5**), a distraught Regan confronts Oswald, whom Goneril has sent with a letter for Edmund. Regan demands to know the letter's contents, but Oswald refuses. Regan wants assurance of Albany's support against the French, which Oswald gives her, remarking that Goneril is a better soldier than her husband. She sends Oswald back to

Goneril to impart the news that Cornwall is dead and that she wishes to marry Edmund; she tells Oswald that if he meets Gloucester, he should kill him. From this point on, the two sisters will be rivals for Edmund's love.

Near Dover, Edgar, still disguised but no longer speaking as a madman, pretends to lead Gloucester to the edge of a high cliff overlooking the sea (**IV.6**). Noting Edgar's changed speech, Gloucester gives him a treasured jewel, bids him to leave, and kneels to pray to the mighty gods. In an aside, Edgar says that he has deceived his father only to save him. Gloucester renounces the unendurable world, blesses his true son, and falls, so he thinks, to his death. When he regains consciousness, Edgar, no longer a beggar but still disguised, convinces Gloucester that he has been miraculously saved. The gods have preserved him from the fiendish beggar who led him to his death. Gloucester, in contrast to his earlier hopelessness and despair, vows henceforth to bear his afflictions stoically.

Lear enters, completely mad and covered with weeds. Edgar laments that so regal a figure should have fallen so far. Lear's ravings do contain some coherence and truth. When king, he had thought himself special, above most people, but his statement "I am not ague-proof" reflects his realization that he is subject to the same pain and suffering as ordinary human beings. In a bitterly ironic defense of adultery, he points out that what appears virtuous is rotten at the core. Gloucester hears Lear's voice and wonders at the fragility of the world. Lear rails against the world's corruption, hypocrisy, and the lack of justice, especially for the poor, and insists that a person does not need eyes to see these failings. Recognizing his old friend at last, Lear cries, "When we are born we cry that we are come / To this great stage of fools."

One of Cordelia's attendants arrives as Lear is inveighing against his sons-in-law. He is to bring Lear to Cordelia, but Lear, still raving, escapes. The gentleman reminds those present that Cordelia is the one daughter "who redeems Nature from the general curse / Which twain have brought her to." The battle between the French and British forces is about to be joined. Gloucester, now calm, asks the ever-gentle gods not to let him be tempted again to take his own life. He allows Edgar to lead him away, thinking him a good man "made tame by fortune's blows."

Oswald now comes upon them and draws his sword to kill Gloucester, but Edgar intervenes and kills Oswald in the ensuing struggle. Before dying, Oswald tells Edgar to give the letters that he is carrying to Edmund. Edgar, reading them, learns that Goneril wants Albany killed so that she can replace him with Edmund. Edgar resolves to use this news later and recognizes Albany's virtue.

In the French camp (**IV.7**), Cordelia meets with Kent, who wants to remain disguised. Lear is brought in, having slept long; gentle music plays. Cordelia embraces him and says, "[L]et this kiss / Repair those violent harms" that the other sisters have done. Lear wakes and believes her to be a heavenly spirit, but slowly regains his senses, his madness vanished. He begins to kneel, but when Cordelia asks for his benediction, he recognizes her and begs her forgiveness for his cruelty and blindness. Kent learns that Edmund is now leader of the slain Cornwall's army and that, according to rumor, Kent and Edgar have fled to Germany. The battle is about to begin.

Near the British camp (**V.1**), Regan, Edmund, and their army await Albany, Goneril, and their soldiers. Regan professes her love for Edmund and jealously questions him about Goneril. When Albany arrives, we learn from Goneril that she would rather lose the battle than lose Edmund to Regan. Albany, showing his true loyalty, is fighting only against the invaders, not against Lear and his supporters. The wicked sisters skirmish over Edmund, whose evil intent is evident by the end of the scene—he will decide which sister is worth more to him on the basis of the battle's results, dispose of Albany, and be unmerciful to Lear and Cordelia. Edgar, still disguised as a peasant, gives Albany the letter from Oswald that reveals Goneril's intentions and tells Albany that, if victorious, he should sound a trumpet to summon an unnamed warrior to confirm the unpleasant story.

Cordelia, leading Lear, crosses a field between the enemy camps with her forces (**V.2**). Edgar leads his father to a sheltering tree and departs. He returns with the news that Lear and

Cordelia have been captured. Gloucester once again despairs. Edgar stoically says, "Men must endure / Their going hence, even as their coming hither; / Ripeness is all."

A triumphant Edmund enters with the captive Lear and Cordelia (**V.3**). Under no circumstances does Lear want to see Goneril and Regan; he is united with his beloved daughter and will be happy to be jailed with her. Edmund instructs a captain to follow them to prison and tells him that if he wishes to advance his career, he must carry out the orders Edmund has written for him.

Albany, Goneril, Regan, and soldiers enter; Albany demands the captives and is furious to find that Edmund has already imprisoned them without a hearing. Both Goneril and Regan protest to Albany, then begin to quarrel bitterly with each other about Edmund. Regan becomes unwell and is taken away. Albany, disgusted with them all and having read the letter Edgar had given him earlier, accuses Edmund of treason and challenges him to fight. A herald sounds the trumpet three times, and Edgar arrives fully armed to denounce Edmund as "false to thy gods, thy brother, and thy father . . . / A most toad-spotted traitor." They fight, and Edmund falls. Goneril spurs Edmund on, and Albany sharply rebukes her, accusing her of monstrous evil. Goneril, desperate, leaves. As Edmund is dying, he confesses to everything that he has been accused of—his noblest act in the play—and asks his challenger to reveal himself, and Edgar does so. Edgar recounts his experiences since his flight and tells how when he finally revealed himself to his father to ask for his blessing before battle, the old earl was so overcome with sadness and joy that he died. In the midst of Edgar's grief, a man rushed in, threw himself on the earl's body, and recounted what had befallen Lear. When Albany's trumpets sounded, Edgar left the man, Kent, paralyzed with sadness.

A gentleman enters with a bloody knife. Goneril has stabbed herself to death, and Regan, poisoned by Goneril, has died. Kent now enters looking for Lear. In the chaos, the king and Cordelia have been forgotten. Edmund, near death, says that contrary to his own nature, there is "[s]ome good I mean to do." He urgently countermands his orders for Cordelia's hanging, which was to look like suicide.

But Edmund's repentance is too late. Lear reenters with Cordelia in his arms, having killed the man who hanged her. She is dead, and Lear's mind once again snaps. Kent finally reveals himself to Lear, but Lear does not seem to recognize him. The action in this last scene is, in Kent's words, "cheerless, dark and deadly." Lear has no more reason to live and dies with Cordelia in his arms.

Albany cedes his power to Kent and Edgar, but Kent, brokenhearted, rejects it, suggesting that he will follow his king to his death. Edgar, who has suffered and endured so much, is left to rule, saying, "The weight of this sad time we must obey." The play, which began with a flourish of trumpets, ends in a sad march. ❖

—Alison Kahn

List of Characters

Lear, king of Britain, is a figure of power and stature at the start of the play. However, his lack of insight, which causes him to misjudge his daughters, leads to his fall from power and descent into madness. Eventually, Lear recognizes his foolishness, but it is too late to save his kingdom, his family, and his life.

Goneril and Regan are the two elder daughters of King Lear, who profess their love for him extravagantly at the beginning of the play, only to betray him. Their treachery toward Lear, each other, and other characters in the play does not go unpunished. Each dies a horrible death brought on by her own scheming.

Cordelia is Lear's youngest and, at the start of the play, most beloved daughter. She is banished because she says she loves the king "according to my bond, no more nor less." Unlike her sisters, Cordelia speaks the truth and exhibits true filial devotion. Much of the play's tragedy stems from Lear's inability to distinguish Cordelia's devotion from her sisters' lies and his inability to save her from death after recognizing her love.

The duke of Albany is Goneril's husband. Although he appears early in the play as a weak character overshadowed by his dominant wife, he later earns our respect by aligning himself against the treachery of Goneril and her cohorts.

The duke of Cornwall is Regan's husband and one of the most pernicious characters of the play. He connives to strip Lear of his power and to seize Gloucester's castle. When Gloucester denounces the plot against Lear, Cornwall gouges out his eyes and crushes them underfoot. In the ensuing struggle with a servant, Cornwall is mortally wounded.

The earl of Gloucester, like Lear, misjudges his children and pays a terrible price. Thrust out of his home, blinded, he finally realizes the love and worth of his steadfast child, Edgar. His actual blinding not only symbolically represents his blindness to his children's characters and its tragic results, but also emphasizes the sad irony that characterizes the play: Only after he loses his sight can Gloucester "see" the truth.

The earl of Kent is banished by Lear because he protests Lear's treatment of Cordelia. Loving the king as a father, Kent resolves to continue to serve Lear—in disguise. Throughout the play, he aids Lear in his struggle against his daughters. At the end of the play, he seems determined to follow Lear to his death.

Edmund, the illegitimate son of Gloucester, is a devious and psychologically complex figure. He schemes to besmirch his brother in his father's eyes and to seize his father's wealth and power. In an interesting parallel to the relationship between Kent and Lear, Edmund becomes the traitorous accomplice of the duke of Cornwall, who comes to be a surrogate father to him. Edmund also becomes the object of both Goneril's and Regan's desire and provokes a fatal jealousy between the two. At the end of the play, in a curious reversal of character, he confesses to his crimes and tries to prevent the hanging of Cordelia, which he ordered.

Edgar, the legitimate son of the earl of Gloucester, is half-brother to Edmund. Like Cordelia, he is rejected by his father after Edmund convinces Gloucester that Edgar is plotting against him. Disguised as the mad beggar Tom, Edgar provides a counterpoint to Lear's insanity and is able to aid his father after Gloucester is blinded. At the play's end, Edgar is left to rule the kingdom, albeit reluctantly and with a heavy heart.

Oswald, Goneril's steward, serves as a messenger between Goneril and Regan. Vain and foppish, he incites trouble and arouses the contempt of others wherever he goes. While attacking Gloucester, he is killed by Edgar.

The fool provides commentary on Lear's actions. He emerges for the first time in Act I, scene 4, and disappears after acting as a judge at Lear's trial of his daughters (III.6). Often the arcane and twisted language of his speeches contains much truth, and his words prophesy events in the play. ❖

Critical Views

SAMUEL JOHNSON ON THE MORAL ISSUES IN *KING LEAR*

[Samuel Johnson (1709–1784), perhaps the greatest British literary figure of the eighteenth century, was a poet, novelist, critic, and biographer of distinction. Perhaps his most celebrated critical work is *Lives of the English Poets* (1779–81). In this extract, taken from the notes to his 1765 edition of Shakespeare, Johnson comments on various moral issues raised by *King Lear*, particularly its conclusion in which Cordelia "perishes in a just cause." Johnson objects to this event and approves of Nahum Tate's 1681 revision of the play in which Cordelia survives.]

The tragedy of Lear is deservedly celebrated among the dramas of Shakespeare. There is perhaps no play which keeps the attention so strongly fixed; which so much agitates our passion and interests our curiosity. The artful involutions of distinct interests, the striking opposition of contrary characters, the sudden changes of fortune, and the quick succession of events, fill the mind with a perpetual tumult of indignation, pity, and hope. There is no scene which does not contribute to the aggravation of the distress or conduct of the action, and scarce a line which does not conduce to the progress of the scene. So powerful is the current of the poet's imagination, that the mind, which once ventures within it, is hurried irresistibly along.

On the seeming improbability of Lear's conduct it may be observed, that he is represented according to histories at that time vulgarly received as true. And perhaps if we turn our thoughts upon the barbarity and ignorance of the age to which this story is referred, it will appear not so unlikely as while we estimate Lear's manners by our own. Such preference of one daughter to another, or resignation of dominion on such conditions, would be yet credible, if told of a petty prince of Guinea or Madagascar. Shakespeare, indeed, by the mention of his earls and dukes, has given us the idea of time more civilized, and of life regulated by softer manners; and the truth is, that though he so nicely discriminates, and so minutely describes the characters of men, he commonly neglects and confounds the characters of ages, by mingling customs ancient and modern, English and foreign.

My learned friend Mr. Warton, who has in the *Adventurer* very minutely criticized this play, remarks, that the instances of cruelty are too savage and shocking, and that the intervention of Edmund destroys the simplicity of the story. These objections may, I think, be answered, by repeating, that the cruelty of the daughters is an historical fact, to which the poet has added very little, having only drawn it into a series by dialogue and action. But I am not able to apologize with equal plausibility for the extrusion of Gloucester's eyes, which seems an act too horrid to be endured in dramatic exhibition, and such as must always compel the mind to relieve its distress by incredulity. Yet let it be remembered that our authour well knew what would please the audience for which he wrote.

The injury done by Edmond to the simplicity of the action is abundantly recompensed by the addition of variety, by the art with which he is made to co-operate with the chief design, and the opportunity which he gives the poet of combining perfidy with perfidy, and connecting the wicked son with the wicked daughters, to impress this important moral, that villany is never at a stop, that crimes lead to crimes, and at last terminate in ruin.

But though this moral be incidentally enforced, Shakespeare has suffered the virtue of Cordelia to perish in a just cause, contrary to the natural ideas of justice, to the hope of the reader, and, what is yet more strange, to the faith of chronicles. Yet this conduct is justified by the Spectator ⟨Joseph Addison⟩, who blames Tate for giving Cordelia success and happiness in his alteration, and declares, that, in his opinion, "the tragedy has lost half its beauty." Dennis has remarked, whether justly or not, that, to secure the favourable reception of *Cato,* "the town was poisoned with much false and abominable criticism," and that endeavours had been used to discredit and decry poetical justice. A play in which the wicked prosper, and the virtuous miscarry, may doubtless be good, because it is a just representation of the common events of human life: but since all reasonable beings naturally love justice, I cannot easily be persuaded, that the observation of justice makes a play worse; or, that if other excellencies are equal, the audience will not always rise better pleased from the final triumph of persecuted virtue.

In the present case the publick has decided. Cordelia, from the time of Tate, has always retired with victory and felicity. And, if my sensations could add anything to the general suffrage, I might relate, that I was many years ago so shocked by Cordelia's death, that I know not whether I ever endured to read again the last scenes of the play till I undertook to revise them as an editor.

—Samuel Johnson, *The Plays of William Shakespeare* (London: J. & R. Tonson, 1765), Vol. 6, p. 158

SAMUEL TAYLOR COLERIDGE ON EDMUND

[Samuel Taylor Coleridge (1772–1834), aside from being one of the greatest British poets of the early nineteenth century, was also a penetrating critic. His most famous critical work is *Biographia Literaria* (1817). In 1819 he delivered a series of lectures on Shakespeare, which were published posthumously in his *Literary Remains* (1836–39). In this extract from that work, Coleridge examines the role of Edmund in *King Lear*.]

⟨. . .⟩ from Lear, the *persona patiens* of his drama, Shakespeare passes without delay to the second in importance, the chief agent and prime mover, and introduces Edmund to our acquaintance, preparing us with the same felicity of judgment, and in the same easy and natural way, for his character in the seemingly casual communication of its origin and occasion. From the first drawing up of the curtain Edmund has stood before us in the united strength and beauty of earliest manhood. Our eyes have been questioning him. Gifted as he is with high advantages of person, and further endowed by nature with a powerful intellect and a strong energetic will, even without any concurrence of circumstances and accident, pride will necessarily be the sin that most easily besets him. But Edmund is also the known and acknowledged son of the princely Gloster: he, therefore, has both the germ of pride, and the conditions best fitted to evolve and ripen it into a predominant feeling. Yet hitherto no reason appears why it should be other than the not unusual pride of person, talent, and birth,—a pride auxiliary, if not akin, to many virtues, and the natural ally of honorable impulses. But alas! in his own presence his own father takes shame to himself for the frank avowal that he is his father,—he has 'blushed so often to acknowledge him that he is now brazed to it!' Edmund hears the circumstances of his birth spoken of with a most degrading and licentious levity,— his mother described as a wanton by her own paramour, and the remembrance of the animal sting, the low criminal gratifications connected with her wantonness and prostituted beauty, assigned as the reason, why 'the whoreson must be acknowledged!' This, and the consciousness of its notoriety; the gnawing conviction that every show of respect is an effort of courtesy, which recalls, while it represses, a contrary feeling;—this is the ever trickling flow of wormwood and gall into the wounds of pride,—the corrosive *virus* which inoculates pride with a venom not its own, with envy, hatred, and a lust for that power which in its blaze of radiance would hide the dark spots on his disc,—with pangs of shame personally undeserved, and therefore felt as wrongs, and with a blind ferment of vindictive working towards the occasions and causes, especially towards a brother, whose stainless birth and lawful honours were the constant remembrances of his own debasement, and were ever in the way to prevent all chance of its being unknown, or overlooked and forgotten. Add to this, that with excellent judgment, and provident for the claims of the moral sense,—for that which, relatively to the drama, is called poetic justice, and as the fittest means for reconciling the feelings of the spectators to the horrors of Gloster's after sufferings,—at least, of rendering them somewhat less unendurable;—(for I will not disguise my conviction, that in this one point the tragic in this play has been urged beyond the outermost mark and *ne plus ultra* of the dramatic)—Shakespeare has precluded all excuse and palliation of the guilt incurred by both the parents of the base-born Edmund, by Gloster's confession that he was at the time a married man, and already blest with a lawful heir of his fortunes. The mournful alienation of brotherly love, occasioned by the law of primogeniture in noble families, or rather by the unnecessary distinctions engrafted thereon, and this in children of the same stock, is still almost proverbial on the continent,—especially, as I know from my own observation, in the South of Europe,—and appears to have been scarcely less common in our own island before the Revolution of 1688, if we may judge from the characters and sentiments so frequent in our elder comedies. There is the younger brother, for instance, in Beaumont and Fletcher's play of the *Scornful Lady,* on the one side, and Oliver in Shakespeare's *As You Like It,* on the other. Need it be said how heavy an aggravation, in such a case, the stain of bastardy must have been, were it only that the younger brother was liable to hear his own dishonour and his mother's infamy related by his father with an excusing shrug of the shoulders, and in a tone betwixt waggery and shame!

—Samuel Taylor Coleridge, "Notes on *King Lear*" (1819), *Literary Remains,* ed. Henry Nelson Coleridge (London: William Pickering, 1836), Vol. 2, pp. 189–92

A. C. BRADLEY ON THE PESSIMISM OF *KING LEAR*

[A. C. Bradley (1851–1935) was the leading British Shakespeare scholar of his time. He taught at the University of Liverpool, the University of Glasgow, and at Oxford University, and wrote *Oxford Lectures on Poetry* (1909) and *A Miscellany* (1929). In this extract, taken from his celebrated book, *Shakespearean Tragedy* (1904), Bradley remarks on what he believes to be the fundamental moral message of *King Lear*—its pessimism in depicting the triumph of evil over good.]

I might almost say that the 'moral' of *King Lear* is presented in the irony of this collocation:

> *Albany:* The gods defend her!
> *Enter Lear with Cordelia dead in his arms.*

The 'gods,' it seems, do *not* show their approval by 'defending' their own from adversity or death, or by giving them power and prosperity. These, on the contrary, are worthless, or worse; it is not on them, but on the renunciation of them, that the gods throw incense. They breed lust, pride, hardness of heart, the insolence of office, cruelty, scorn, hypocrisy, contention, war, murder, self-destruction. The whole story beats this indictment of prosperity into the brain. Lear's great speeches in his madness proclaim it like the curses of Timon on life and man. But here, as in *Timon,* the poor and humble are, almost without exception, sound and sweet at heart, faithful and pitiful. And here adversity, to the blessed in spirit, is blessed. It wins fragrance from the crushed flower. It melts in aged hearts sympathies which prosperity had frozen. It purges the soul's sight by blinding that of the eyes. Throughout that stupendous Third Act the good are seen growing better through suffering, and the bad worse through success. The warm castle is a room in hell, the storm-swept heath a sanctuary. The judgment of this world is a lie; its goods, which we covet, corrupt us; its ills, which break our bodies, set our souls free;

> Our means secure us, and our mere defects
> Prove our commodities.

Let us renounce the world, hate it, and lose it gladly. The only real thing in it is the soul, with its courage, patience, devotion. And nothing outward can touch that.

This, if we like to use the word, is Shakespeare's 'pessimism' in *King Lear.* As we have seen, it is not by any means the whole spirit of the tragedy, which presents the world as a place where heavenly good grows side by side with evil, where extreme evil cannot long endure, and where all that survives the storm is good, if not great. But still this strain of thought, to which the world appears as the kingdom of evil and therefore worthless, is in the tragedy, and may well be the record of many hours of exasperated feeling and troubled brooding. Pursued further and allowed to dominate, it would destroy the tragedy; for it is necessary to tragedy that we should feel that suffering and death do matter greatly, and that happiness and life are not to be renounced as worthless. Pursued further, again, it leads to the idea that the world, in that obvious appearance of it which tragedy cannot dissolve without dissolving itself, is illusive. And its tendency towards this idea is traceable in *King Lear,* in the shape of the notion that this 'great world' is transitory, or 'will wear out to nought' like the little world called 'man' (IV. vi. 137), or that humanity will destroy itself.

—A. C. Bradley, *Shakespearean Tragedy* (London: Macmillan, 1904), pp. 326–28

LEO TOLSTOY ON THE FAILINGS OF *KING LEAR*

[Leo Tolstoy (1828–1910), one of the greatest novelists in Russian literature and the author of *War and Peace* (1863–69), wrote a polemic against Shakespeare toward the end of his life. He singled out *King Lear* for disapproval, perhaps because its depiction of evil's triumph over good offended his Christian sensibilities. In this extract, Tolstoy points out what he believes to be the many failings and improbabilities of the play, especially in its characterizations.]

In *King Lear* the persons represented are indeed placed externally in opposition to the outward world, and they struggle with it. But their strife does not flow from the natural course of events nor from their own characters, but is quite arbitrarily established by the author, and therefore can not produce on the reader the illusion which represents the essential condition of art.

Lear has no necessity or motive for his abdication; also, having lived all his life with his daughters, has no reason to believe the words of the two elders and not the truthful statement of the youngest; yet upon this is built the whole tragedy of his position.

Similarly unnatural is the subordinate action: the relation of Gloucester to his sons. The positions of Gloucester and Edgar flow from the circumstance that Gloucester, just like Lear, immediately believes the coarsest untruth and does not even endeavor to inquire of his injured son whether what he is accused of be true, but at once curses and banishes him. The fact that Lear's relations with his daughters are the same as those of Gloucester to his sons makes one feel yet more strongly that in both cases the relations are quite arbitrary, and do not flow from the characters nor the natural course of events. Equally unnatural, and obviously invented, is the fact that all through the tragedy Lear does not recognize his old courtier, Kent, and therefore the relations between Lear and Kent fail to excite the sympathy of the reader or spectator. The same, in a yet greater degree, holds true of the position of Edgar, who, unrecognized by any one, leads his blind father and persuades him that he has leapt off a cliff, when in reality Gloucester jumps on level ground.

These positions, into which the characters are placed quite arbitrarily, are so unnatural that the reader or spectator is unable not only to sympathize with their sufferings but even to be interested in what he reads or sees. This in the first place.

Secondly, in this, as in the other dramas of Shakespeare, all the characters live, think, speak, and act quite unconformably with the given time and place. The action of *King Lear* takes place 800 years B.C., and yet the characters are placed in conditions possible only in the Middle Ages: participating in the drama are kings, dukes, armies, and illegitimate children, and gentlemen, courtiers, doctors, farmers, officers, soldiers, and knights with vizors, etc. It is possible that such anachronisms (with which Shakespeare's dramas abound) did not injure the possibility of illusion in the sixteenth century and the beginning of the seventeenth, but in our time it is no longer possible to follow with interest the development of events which one knows could not take place in the conditions which the author describes in detail. The artificiality of the positions, not flowing from the natural course of events, or from the nature of the characters, and their want of conformity with time and space, is further increased by those coarse embellishments which are continually added by Shakespeare and intended to appear particularly touching. The extraordinary storm during which King Lear roams about the heath, or the grass which for some reason he puts on his head—like Ophelia in *Hamlet*—or Edgar's attire, or the fool's speeches, or the appearance of the helmeted horseman, Edgar—all these effects not only fail to enhance the impression, but produce an opposite effect. "Man sieht die Absicht und man wird verstimmt," as Goethe says. It often happens that even during these obviously intentional efforts after effect, as, for instance, the dragging out by the legs of half a dozen corpses, with which all Shakespeare's tragedies terminate, instead of feeling fear and pity, one is tempted rather to laugh.

—Leo Tolstoy, *On Shakespeare*, tr. V. Tchertkoff and I. F. M. (New York: Funk & Wagnalls, 1906), pp. 48–51

Lily B. Campbell on the Vanity of King Lear

[Lily B. Campbell (1883–1967) was a literary critic who wrote *Shakespeare's "Histories": Mirrors of Elizabethan Policy* (1947) and *Divine Poetry and Drama in Sixteenth-Century England* (1959). In this extract from *Shakespeare's Tragic Heroes* (1930), Campbell argues that Lear's pride and self-love give rise to his tragic end.]

That it is self-love that makes a man susceptible to flattery is shown in the next speech, but the speech indicates much more than a susceptibility to flattery. In self-love and injured self-esteem anger takes its rise, as we have seen. To Cordelia's tempered and reasonable speech, the aged King breaks out at once in intemperate and almost frenzied anger:

> Let it be so; thy truth, then, be thy dower!
> For, by the sacred radiance of the sun,
> The mysteries of Hecate, and the night;
> By all the operation of the orbs
> From whom we do exist, and cease to be;
> Here I disclaim all my paternal care,
> Propinquity and property of blood,
> And as a stranger to my heart and me
> Hold thee, from this, forever. The barbarous Scythian,
> Or he that makes his generation messes
> To gorge his appetite, shall to my bosom
> Be as well neighbour'd, piti'd, and reliev'd,
> As thou my sometime daughter.   (I.i. 110–22)

Then it is that another friend dares to speak to dissuade from unjust action, but the good Kent's interruption is checked by Lear's

> Come not between the dragon and his wrath.
> I lov'd her most, and thought to set my rest
> On her kind nursery. (I.i. 124–6)

And thus in the beginning of his wrath we see Lear demonstrating what we know to have been an accepted principle, that a man is angered by an injury to his self-esteem, that he is soonest angered when that respect in which he has thought himself most worthy seems to be disregarded, that he is soonest angry with friends, with those who have previously treated him becomingly and now change, and with those who do not appreciate his kindness. Cordelia, most loved and most loving heretofore, to whom he intended the greatest favours, is at once the easy victim of the aged Lear. And as is the manner of the angry man, he at once seeks to have revenge, to show his power, and to injure the one from whom he conceives himself to have received an injury. At once he adds to the dowers of his two flattering daughters all the third that should have been Cordelia's. It must be noted, however, that while he gives away the burdens of the state, he retains

> The name, and all the addition to a king;

and thus we see that pride will still be panoplied with the trappings of a king. His monthly progress between the divided halves of his kingdom with his extensive retinue evidently pleases him as he pictures it. His pride and self-esteem are so mingled with his anger and his desire for revenge in this speech that they become one.

Again Kent will show that he is a true friend by attempting to check the rashness of his king, but Lear again rebuffs him:

> The bow is bent and drawn; make from the shaft. (I.i. 145)

Now Kent becomes the man of righteous anger, angry not at the doer, but at the deed; further, he is the true friend opposing himself to the flatterer as he replies:

> . . . be Kent unmannerly
> When Lear is mad. What wouldst thou do, old man?
> Thinks thou that duty shall have dread to speak
> When power to flattery bows? (I.i. 147–50)

And he begs Lear to check his "hideous rashness", even as he pleads the love of Cordelia. And even to the King's threat of his life, he will not yield his right to try to protect him from himself. Even as the King lays his hand upon his sword, Kent exclaims again:

> Kill thy physician, and thy fee bestow
> Upon the foul disease. Revoke thy gift;
> Or, whilst I can vent clamour from my throat,
> I'll tell thee thou dost evil. (I.i. 165–8)

And now, just as Lear has turned in his pride to try to revenge himself for the injury to his self-esteem inflicted by Cordelia's refusal to offer flattering vows and promises, he turns likewise at once in pride and outrageous anger to revenge himself on his most loyal friend, who likewise has refused to play the part of flatterer but has instead insisted upon trying to save him from evil and folly by telling him the truth. At once Lear shows his power in ordering the faithful Kent to turn his "hated back" upon his kingdom by the sixth day, the forfeit of his life to be exacted if he fail to accept his brutal banishment.

> —Lily B. Campbell, *Shakespeare's Tragic Heroes: Slaves of Passion* (Cambridge: Cambridge University Press, 1930), pp.185–87

GEORGE ORWELL ON TOLSTOY, LEAR, AND RENUNCIATION

[George Orwell (1903–1950) was a leading British novelist and political activist of his generation, today best known for the novels *Animal Farm* (1945) and *Nineteen Eighty-Four* (1949). In this extract, Orwell comments on Leo Tolstoy's reading of *King Lear* and then argues that the theme of the play is renunciation.]

Lear is one of the minority of Shakespeare's plays that are unmistakably *about* something. As Tolstoy justly complains, much rubbish has been written about Shakespeare as a philosopher, as a psychologist, as a "great moral teacher," and whatnot. Shakespeare was not a systematic thinker, his most serious thoughts are uttered irrelevantly or indirectly, and we do not know to what extent he wrote with a "purpose" or even how much of the work attributed to him was actually written by him. In the sonnets he never even refers to the plays as part of his achievement, though he does make what seems to be a half-ashamed allusion to his career as an actor. It is perfectly possible that he looked on at least half of his plays as mere potboilers and hardly bothered about purpose or probability so long as he could patch up something, usually from stolen material, which would more or less hang together on the stage. However, that is not the whole story. To begin with, as Tolstoy himself points out, Shakespeare has a habit of thrusting uncalled-for general reflections into the mouths of his characters. This is a serious fault in a dramatist, but it does not fit in with Tolstoy's picture of Shakespeare as a vulgar hack who has no opinions of his own and merely wishes to produce the greatest effect with the least trouble. And more than this, about a dozen of his plays, written for the most part later than 1600, do unquestionably have a meaning and even a moral. They revolve around a central subject which in some cases can be reduced to a single word. For example, *Macbeth* is about ambition, *Othello* is about jealousy, and *Timon of Athens* is about money. The subject of *Lear* is renunciation, and it is only by being wilfully blind that one can fail to understand what Shakespeare is saying.

Lear renounces his throne but expects everyone to continue treating him as a king. He does not see that if he surrenders power, other people will take advantage of his weakness: also that those who flatter him most grossly, i.e. Regan and Goneril, are exactly the ones who will turn against him. The moment he finds that he can no longer make people obey him as he did before, he falls into a rage which Tolstoy describes as "strange and unnatural," but which in fact is perfectly in character. In his madness and despair, he passes through two moods which again are natural enough in his circumstances, though in one of them it is probable that he is being used partly as a mouth-piece for Shakespeare's own opinions. One is the mood of disgust in which Lear repents, as it were, for having been a king, and grasps for the first time the rottenness of formal justice and vulgar morality. The other is a mood of impotent fury in which he wreaks imaginary revenges upon those who have wronged him. "To have a thousand with red burning spits come hissing in upon 'em!", and:

> It were a delicate stratagem to shoe
> A troop of horse with felt: I'll put't in proof;
> And when I have stol'n upon these sons-in-law,
> Then kill, kill, kill, kill, kill!

Only at the end does he realize, as a sane man, that power, revenge, and victory are not worth while:

> No, no, no, no! Come, let's away to prison . . .
>   and we'll wear out
> In a wall'd prison, packs and sects of great ones
> That ebb and flow by the moon.

But by the time he makes this discovery it is too late, for his death and Cordelia's are already decided on. That is the story, and, allowing for some clumsiness in the telling, it is a very good story.

—George Orwell, "Lear, Tolstoy and the Fool" (1947), *Collected Essays, Journalism and Letters of George Orwell,* ed. Sonia Orwell and Ian Angus (New York: Harcourt Brace Jovanovich, 1968), Vol. 4, pp. 295–96

ROBERT BECHTOLD HEILMAN ON AGE IN *KING LEAR*

[Robert Bechtold Heilman (b. 1906) is a former professor of English at the University of Washington. Among his many books on drama are *Magic in the Web: Action and Language in* Othello (1977) and *The Ways of the World: Comedy and Society* (1978). In this extract from his study of *King Lear* (1948), Heilman explores a twofold view of age in the play.]

In *King Lear* we find, then, a twofold view of age. On the one hand age is allied with Nature: it has a certain position to which a certain response is obligatory. If man adheres to the order of the whole, he cannot withhold from age what is its due from an ordered humanity—respect and loving-kindness. On the other hand, age becomes an isolated fact whose significance lies only in its relevance to the situations of those who must deal with it, and they are under no obligation to apply it to any other standard than that of interest. Their view is pragmatic; the pragmatists are Goneril, Regan, and Edmund. Nearly all other characters in the play regard age as having established rights within the realm of humanity. These characters are those who understand Nature as *nomos,* and in whom, as we shall see, there is a strong religious sense.

Age is first of all a subject of which Lear himself is very conscious, and by means of which we can trace certain changes in his consciousness. At the start, age is to him simply a time of rest:

> To shake all cares and business from our age,
> Conferring them on younger strengths, while we
> Unburthen'd crawl toward death.   (I.i, 40–42)

Then there is the first trace of youth-age counterpoint. Lear speaks of Cordelia's "young love" (I.i, 85), and in the statement of his subsequent disappointment in her there is a carry-over, with a pun, of the same idea: "So young, and so untender?" (I.i, 108) What he says of Cordelia is inevitably called up by a part of his curse on Goneril: may she have a "child of spleen" that will "stamp wrinkles in her brow of youth" (I.iv, 304–306). Lear's inquiry about the disguised Kent's age, and Kent's answer (I.iv, 39–42) continue the theme. What now begins to come over Lear, as understanding of Goneril and Regan is forced upon him, is the realization that the position of age is not exactly the small assured portion of human privilege that he once thought, and here he finds what is an extra twist of the horrifying violation of nature. He says he is "a poor old man, / As full of grief as age" (II.iv, 275–76), a "despis'd old man" (III.ii, 20), "So old and white as this" (III.ii, 24), and "Your old kind father" (III.iv, 20). At one level this repetition of *old* is an index of self-pity, as various critics have seen; in either sentimentality or violence, Lear can fall very short of dignity and manliness. He is never whitewashed. Yet at the same time the recurrence of *old* has another effect, one produced by poetic suggestion: it is a way of expressing incredulity that such experiences could happen to an *old* man. That is, to age the "offices of nature" (II.iv, 181) are more than ever due; age has certain prerogatives in the order of things; viciousness to age is therefore a rupture in nature. Since this is Lear's unexpressed assumption, it is no wonder that in the quieter mood which precedes the final scene, Lear is inclined to accept age as almost the equivalent of folly. "I am a very foolish, fond old man" he says (IV.vii, 60), and "I am old and foolish" (IV.vii, 84).

Now, Lear's conviction that age strengthens "nature," so to speak—that is, especially obligates others in performance of duty—is shared by many of the other characters. They regard age as of itself exacting compassion. Kent calls Lear "the old kind King" (III.i, 28); Albany calls him a "gracious aged man" (IV.ii, 41) and says he will assign power to "this old majesty" (V.iii, 299). Cordelia says French arms are incited by love "and our ag'd father's right" (IV.iv, 28). When he is about to be tortured by Regan and Cornwall, Gloucester can speak of Lear's "poor old eyes" (III.vii, 57) and "poor old heart" (62). Gloucester has already seen Edgar's imagined injury to him in terms of his age: he has told Regan that his "old heart is crack'd, it's crack'd!" (II.i, 92) Now, when Cornwall moves toward him, this awareness of age bursts forth into Gloucester's climactic cry of anguish: "He that will think to live till he be old, / Give me some help" (III.vii, 69–70). His prayer exactly parallels an earlier one of Lear's:

> O heavens,
> If you do love old men, if your sweet sway
> Allow obedience, if yourselves are old,
> Make it your cause! Send down, and take my part!
>
> (II.iv, 192–95)

When Kent, deprecating the stocks, says to Cornwall, "I am too old to learn" (II.ii, 134), he speaks for Lear as well as himself. All the old men do learn, of course; what Kent really does is to make a choral commentary on the destructive difficulty of the learning process. The educating experiences through which Lear and Gloucester have gone are "out of nature." So, while at one level we have the irony of old age's receiving treatment the opposite of what it might expect, at another we have an enrichment of the nature pattern: the stress upon age, and upon its due, is a way of reinforcing our sense of a Nature of things to which violence has been done. Yet through some instrument or other Nature continues to function: it is very effective, after all the stress on injured age, to have Gloucester, after his blinding, led by an Old Man who has been his and his father's tenant "these fourscore years" (IV.i, 14). In the Old Man's service we have a symbol of order at the cosmic level, and, at the same time, of the continued sustaining power of the old order which seems to be going to pieces. This is one of the hints of a clash between orders, a historical crisis, of which we shall see more.

—Robert Bechtold Heilman, This Great Stage: Image and Structure in King Lear (Baton Rouge: Louisiana State University Press, 1948), pp. 135–38

IRVING RIBNER ON REGENERATION IN *KING LEAR*

[Irving Ribner (1921–1972), formerly chairman of the English department at the State University of New York at Stony Brook, wrote *William Shakespeare: An Introduction to His Life, Times, and Theatre* (1969) and *Jacobean Tragedy: The Quest for Moral Order* (1962). In this extract, Ribner argues that the fundamental theme in *King Lear* is regeneration and the "universal role of man in conflict with evil."]

In *King Lear* Shakespeare's emphasis is upon the process of human regeneration, the self-knowledge, penance, and expiation for sin upon which he had touched only lightly in the final scene of *Othello.* That Shakespeare now chose for his hero an old man was thematically appropriate, for his concern is with a spiritual rebirth for which man never can grow too old. Shakespeare juxtaposes dramatically the physical age of his hero against the new manhood he attains through suffering; he affirms that Lear's four score years of pride and self-deception were merely the prelude to life, not true to life at all.

The cruelty and the suffering in *King Lear* have led many critics to call the play a secular tragedy in which Shakespeare offers neither insight into the cause of human suffering nor hope for man other than in stoical submission. Such a view tends to take the play's savagery out of its context in the larger design, to see *Lear* as a disordered mass of impressions, rather than as a neatly unified whole, every element of which is designed to give dramatic form to a thematic statement. The suffering of Lear and Gloucester is presented with all the immediate intensity of which Shakespeare is capable in order to emphasize that the process of regeneration is a purgatorial one. If Shakespeare is to assert the power of man to overcome evil, the forces of evil must be shown in their most uncompromising terms. *King Lear* is a triumph of dramatic construction which in its total effect, like *Hamlet* and *Othello* affirms justice in the world, which it sees as a harmonious system ruled by a benevolent God.

All the elements of *King Lear* are shaped by the theme of regeneration which dominates the whole. To find a fitting dramatic form for this new theme, Shakespeare had to extend and develop the pattern for tragedy he had evolved in *Othello.* Again he availed himself of the morality play formula which was so much a part of the dramatic tradition of his age. The didactic and homiletic tradition of medieval drama afforded tools by which Shakespeare might shape a complex of action to reflect the universal role of man in conflict with evil. To reinforce his theme Shakespeare now employed a new device, the parallel tragedy of Gloucester. The double action offers us another hero who is Lear on a slightly lower social plane, and his career by paralleling closely that of Lear reinforces the universal validity of the play's theme.

All the characters perform symbolic functions. The primary focus is upon Lear, and to a lesser extent upon Gloucester; they stand together for humanity at large. The other characters serve secondary supporting functions, each symbolic of some force of good or evil acting upon humanity. The theatre of the action is not only the single world of man, but also its corresponding planes in the scheme of creation: the family, the state, and the physical universe. The universality of theme is reinforced by the vagueness of the place setting; the audience watches not only Lear's little kingdom, but the great world itself.

—Irving Ribner, *Patterns in Shakespearean Tragedy* (London: Methuen, 1960), pp.116–17

JOHN HOLLOWAY ON EVIL IN *KING LEAR*

[John Holloway (b. 1920) is a fellow of Queen's College, Cambridge, and a widely published poet and critic. Among his works are *The Proud Knowledge: Poetry, Insight and Self 1620–1920* (1977) and *Narrative and Structure: Exploratory Essays* (1979). In this extract from his study of Shakespeare's tragedies (1961), Holloway comments on evil in *King Lear* and contrasts it to the presentation of evil in *Macbeth*.]

Disruption in the kingdom, disruption in the family, linked by tradition, were facets of that universal disruption of Nature, that Descent into Chaos, which for millennia had been a standing dread of mankind and at the same time one of mankind's convictions about providential history in the future.

King Lear is an exploration of this potentiality to quite a different degree from, say, *Macbeth*. The nadir of that play, the point at which Macbeth's own evil nature seems to diffuse evil throughout his whole country, falls short of what happens even at the start of *Lear*. In *Macbeth* the evil emanates from one man (or one couple) quite alone. In *Lear* it seems, from the first, like an infection spreading everywhere, affecting a general change in human nature, even in all nature. Those, like Kent and Cordelia, who stand out against its progress, manifest its influence even in doing so: as if Burton's 'riot' could be countered (which may be true, indeed) only by riot of another kind. The disease is general; antidotes are helpless or non-existent; the course must be run.

In its details, the play sometimes displays an extraordinary realism. Lear's hesitation before he demands to see the supposedly sick Duke of Cornwall and his inability to believe that his messenger has been set in the stocks, Edgar's impersonation of the peasant, the whole dialogue in Act V scene iii between Albany, Edmund, Goneril and Regan, are all instances of unforgettable rightness and richness in catching the complex and individualized movements of minds vehemently working and intently engaged. Yet for a sense of the play as a whole this has less weight than what is almost its opposite: an action deliberately stylized so that its generic quality and it decisive movement should stand out more than its human detail. This is true, notably, of the division of the kingdom with which the play opens. We must see this as stylized not merely in its quality as it takes its place on the stage, but in how it points forward. Time and again this kind of event occurs in contemporary drama (*Gorboduc, The Misfortunes of Arthur, Selimus, Woodstock, Locrine* are examples). Its status as decisively misguided or evil is not in doubt; and it is the established sign or first step in a movement which threatens chaos or actually brings it. The direction and nature of what is to happen in *Lear* need not be inferred by the spectator through his detailed response to the behaviour and dialogue of the actors. Richly as it may be confirmed and elaborated in these things, its essence stands starkly before him in the stylization of a known kind of opening event. The intricate complication of the story, the detailed characterization, do nothing to obscure what is clear in the almost folk-tale quality of how the play begins. '*We have seen* the best of our time.'

Those words of Gloucester are essentially dynamic words, and this movement and dynamic ought to be seen in an aspect of *King Lear* which has been so much discussed that here it need not be discussed in full: its imagery. That the characters in the play are repeatedly likened to the lower orders of creation, for example, gives no mere general or pervasive tinge to the work, and embodies no merely general idea about humanity at large. It cannot be found in the opening scene. It arrives as the action begins to move, and becomes dominant as the quality of life which it embodies becomes dominant in the play. Just as it is not enough for Professor ⟨Kenneth⟩ Muir to say that the plot of Lear 'expressed the theme of the parent-child relationship'—for it expressed no mere problem or issue, because it depicts a particular movement which begins when that relationship fails in a definite way—so it is not enough for him to refer to 'the prevalence of animal imagery' and to add merely: 'This imagery is partly designed to show man's place in the Chain of Being, and to bring out the subhuman nature of the evil characters, partly to show man's weakness compared with the animals, and partly to compare human life to the life of the jungle.' The hedge-sparrow that fed the cuckoo, the sea-monster that is less hideous than ingratitude in a child, ingratitude itself sharper than a serpent's tooth, the wolfish visage of Goneril, are not scattered throughout the play as mere figurative embodiments of those discursive or philosophical interests. They burst upon the audience all together, at the close of Act I. If they throw out some general and discursive suggestion about 'human life', that is far less prominent than how they qualify the phase of the action which comes at that point, crowding the audience's imagination, surrounding the human characters with the sub-human creatures whose appearance they are fast and eagerly assuming.

—John Holloway, *The Story of the Night: Studies in Shakespeare's Major Tragedies* (London: Routledge & Kegan Paul, 1961), pp. 79–81

JOSEPHINE WATERS BENNETT ON LEAR'S MADNESS

[Josephine Waters Bennett (1899–1975) was a professor of English at Hunter College. She wrote Measure for Measure *as Royal Entertainment* (1966) and coedited *Studies in the English Renaissance Drama* (1959). In this extract, Bennett explores Act III of the play, in which it becomes clear that Lear has gone mad.]

In spite of the preparation for Lear's madness by his own and others' suggestions of it, and in spite of the three clear symptoms of derangement in III.iv, no critic, so far as I can find, has observed that the chief function of this scene at the hovel is to establish that Lear is mad. Even Coleridge, who does not seem to have felt that the madness must be progressive, says that "this scene *ends* with the first symptoms of positive derangement", and that Lear appears "in full madness in the sixth scene". Those who feel that the insanity must be climactic emphasize Kent's apologetic, "His wits *begin* t'unsettle" (iv.153), and Gloucester's reply, "Thou say'st the king *grows* mad", but at the opening of scene vi, only twenty-five lines later, Kent says, "*All* the power of his wits *have given way* to his impatience." If we are to weigh words and tenses, we cannot ignore Kent's *all* and *have given* while emphasizing *begins* and *grows*.

Whatever readers of the play, and criticism based on reading, may contend, it seems obvious that Shakespeare intended his auditors to understand that Lear goes mad in III.iv and is mad when he appears next in scene vi. If the play is a properly constructed Elizabethan tragedy, the climax, or point of no return in the struggle which makes the plot, should come in this scene. Scenes iii, v, and vii bring the Gloucester plot to its climax of horror. Scenes ii, iv, and vi are concerned with Lear. Scene ii shows us his defiance of the storm and his self-pity:

> I am a man
> More sinned against than sinning   (III.ii, 58–59)

and his premonition of madness: "My wits begin to turn." In the next scene in which he appears we see him go mad, and in the opening of scene vi Kent says that "All the power of his wits have given away to his impatience." The problem is not, therefore, *whether* he is mad in III.iv, but *why* he is mad, and what dramatic purposes are served by the two further exhibitions of his madness.

Kent's clear and emphatic assertion that Lear is now completely mad prepares the audience for the uninhibited exhibition of Lear's inner conflict, and in successive speeches we are shown his pride, his furious desire for revenge, his attempt to use "justice" to get that revenge, and his self-pity. When the Fool proposes his conundrum, "Prithee, nuncle, tell me whether a madman be a gentleman or a yeoman?" Lear understands that the quip is aimed at him and replies proudly, "A king, a king." The Fool supplies the correct answer, but Lear's mind is obsessed with his passionate desire for revenge:

> To have a thousand with red burning spits
> Come hizzing in upon 'em—   (ll. 15–16)

This furious desire to "punish home", to torture, is as shocking as Lear's earlier cursing of Goneril. It is, in fact, as savage in wish as the blinding of Gloucester is in deed. This is the cause of Lear's madness, his bitter, futile resentment, his frustrated will which has driven him to insane hatred.

In the play-within-a-play which follows, the Fool and Edgar humor Lear by acting the parts he assigns to them, but they also comment, in asides, on the pity of Lear's insanity; as when Edgar says, "Bless thy five wits!" and "My tears begin to take his part so much / They mar my counterfeiting" (i.e. acting the part of the judge). Lear's mind fluctuates from excitement over the imagined escape of Goneril to the abyss of self-pity in which he imagined his dogs behaving like his daughters,

> The little dogs and all,
> Tray, Blanch, and Sweetheart—see, they bark at me.   (ll. 61–62)

The next moment he is ready to anatomize Regan to find out, "Is there any cause in nature that makes these hard hearts?" Then, forgetting what he is about, he tells Tom, "You, sir, I entertain for one of my hundred; only I do not like the fashion of your garments. You will say they are Persian; but let them be changed." This is an echo of his grievance (my hundred), and of his delusion that Tom is an ancient philosopher (end of sc. iv). It serves to remind the audience that he is mad. The reminder is reinforced, a few lines later by Kent's words, "trouble him not; his wits are gone."

This scene gives us, not a further degree of insanity, but a clear exposition of the internal cause of Lear's madness. Balked pride, humiliation, impotence, and self-pity have worn him out and in the midst of this scene he falls asleep out of sheer exhaustion. We do not see him again until IV.vi. Before we turn to that scene it seems necessary to consider for a moment the function of the Fool.

Because of the Nature of Lear's internal conflict, his stubborn resistance to the humbling forces unleashed against him, the devices of self-revelation so commonly used by Elizabethan dramatists—soliloquies, asides, and conversations with a confidant—are not open to Shakespeare in this play. Lear cannot debate within himself nor surrender his pride so far as to confide in anyone. The condition of his ordeal is that he cannot recognize his own weakness and dependence on others, and so he cannot admit the self-doubt and soul-searching and regret which Hamlet and Macbeth give voice to. Shakespeare was, therefore, faced with the technical problem of giving dramatic expression to one side of the internal conflict in Lear. Kent's vigorous protest is effectively silenced in the first scene. Lear himself could not express regret or self-reproach until the tempest within was over, until the struggle of his will against all the forces of life had passed its crisis and he had come to know himself.

It is the solution of this problem of how to keep before the audience Lear's guilt and folly that produced the Fool, perhaps Shakespeare's boldest stroke of genius. The tradition of the allowed Fool made him possible. Because of his unique position he could serve as a chorus representing the voice of wisdom. He has been described as a kind of external conscience, but it is not Lear's injustice but his folly that the Fool harps on. He does, however, in some respects, act not only as a reminder, but as a representative of Cordelia, appealing to Lear's affections by his doglike devotion, depending on him for protection, and so keeping Lear human in that part of the play where Cordelia cannot appear, keeping the audience reminded of her and of Lear's capacity for love.

—Josephine Waters Bennett, "The Storm Within: The Madness of Lear," *Shakespeare Quarterly* 13, No. 2 (Spring 1962): 142–44

[William Rosen (b. 1926) is the author of *Shakespeare and the Craft of Tragedy* (1964), from which the following extract is taken. Here, Rosen studies the character of King Lear and the nature of kingship in the play.]

In *King Lear*, though the king's character is not sketched before he appears on stage, he nevertheless comes immediately into a certain frame of reference, not through the technique of prefiguring, but through his own exalted status. For an Elizabethan audience particularly, his figure would expand in minds to encompass a whole context of values. The person of Lear is from the very beginning associated with great honor, for he can be viewed as the highest human embodiment of all the elements which give order and dignity to society: he is king of his nation, father of his family, and he is an old man. Hence the respect which he should command is triply compounded. Now it is not absolutely necessary to turn to Elizabethan concepts of kingship or order to understand the respect and honor due to one who is king, who is father, and who is old. Such ideas have not disappeared with the passing of some three hundred and fifty years. However, a brief reference to Elizabethan attitudes is appropriate here because the respect due to Lear is central to the play.

Certainly "kingship" had an evocative power for Elizabethans. There is divinity that hedges a king—we find this idea reiterated in much of the writing of the age. Furthermore, the correspondence between the power of the king and that of the father was an Elizabethan commonplace illustrating the order of a universe in which, as God governed all, so kings ruled states, and fathers, families. In *The French Academie,* whose popularity is attested by its many English editions from 1586 to 1614, La Primaudaye makes an observation that might serve as a commentary on *King Lear:*

> Everie house must be ruled by the eldest, as by a king, who by nature commandeth over everie part of the house, and they obey him for the good preservation thereof. . . . This commandment over, is called roiall, bicause he that begetteth, commandeth by love, and by the prerogative of age, which is a kind of

kingly commanding. . . . The father is the true image of the great & soveraign God, the universal father of al things.

Thus the ordered family, the private life of a nation, is a mirroring in miniature of the ordered hierarchy of public society; and analogies between the king and his subjects and the father and his children prevailed.

It is within such a context that we first see King Lear: his figure activates in the minds of an audience patterns of value of which he is the embodiment. His formal entrance highlights all the dignity and authority associated with kingship. The set of notes sounded, the "sennet," ushers in the concrete symbol of royalty, "enter one bearing a coronet"; and the stage directions give the precise order of entrance which accords with the prerogatives of rank: "King Lear, Cornwall, Albany, Goneril, Regan, Cordelia, and Attendants." On the Elizabethan stage this would be a stately procession of splendor, Lear the central figure in a crowded scene. All are Lear's subjects, dependent upon him.

Lear's stature is even further magnified in his first extended pronouncement in which he tells of his intentions to divest himself of "rule, / Interest of territory, cares of state" (I.i.50), for we see him in the role of public and private figure at one and the same time. Because he is king, his actions in dividing the realm have public consequences affecting the destiny of the state; as benefactor to his children in this division, his actions affect the private life of the family as well. And yet, though the figure of the king bodies forth the ideal, the highest good of family and nation, it is important to see that in this scene Shakespeare presents his central character as an ironist would; and in this way: that the audience does not fully engage its sympathies with Lear or those who oppose him since the dramatist supports the values which Lear represents while revealing the king's misguided position.

—William Rosen, *Shakespeare and the Craft of Tragedy* (Cambridge, MA: Harvard University Press, 1964), pp. 1–3

[Northrop Frye (1912–1991) was one of the most important literary critics of his generation. Among his many books are *Anatomy of Criticism* (1957), *Fables of Identity: Studies in Poetic Mythology* (1963), *A Natural Perspective: The Development of Shakespearean Comedy and Romance* (1965), and *The Great Code: The Bible and Literature* (1982). For many years he was University Professor and vice chancellor of Victoria College at the University of Toronto. In this extract from *Fools of Time* (1967), his study of Shakespeare's tragedies, Frye sees *King Lear* as exemplifying the distinction between tragedy and melodrama.]

King Lear has been called a purgatorial tragedy, and if that means a structure even remotely like Dante's *Purgatorio,* we should expect to see, as we see in Dante, existence being taken over and shaped by a moral force. Our understanding of the tragedy, then, would have that qualified response in it that is inseparable from a moral or conceptual outlook. It is true that Lear has suffered terribly, but he has thereby gained, etc. Suffering is inevitable in the nature of things, yet, etc. But of course, Lear is not saying anything like this at the end of the play: what he is saying is that Cordelia is gone, and will never, never come back to him. Perhaps he thinks that she is coming back to life again, and dies of an unbearable joy. But we do not see this: all we see is an old man dying of unbearable pain. The hideous wrench of agony which the death of Cordelia gives the play is too much a part of the play even to be explained as inexplicable. And whatever else may be true, the vision of absurd anguish in which the play ends is certainly true.

We began this discussion by establishing a distinction between authentic tragedy and melodrama. By melodrama I mean a dramatic vision that confirms the audience's stock moral responses: that achieves comedy primarily by applauding the hero and tragedy primarily by punishing the villain. Such a dramatic vision is aesthetic in the perverted Kierkegaardian sense of externalizing man's ethical freedom. In a sense it is anti-tragic, providing as it does a justification for a tragic action that comes from something outside tragedy, and so, really, explaining tragedy away. In authentic tragedy what we see as external to us is, first of all, the order of nature, with its servomechanism the wheel of fortune. Nature and fortune, when seen from the point of view of the human situation, constitute a vision of absurdity and anguish, what design is in them being unintelligible to human imagination, human emotions, and ultimately to human moral instincts. Introducing thunder as the voice of disapproving divinity in Tourneur is melodramatic, in the sense that it presents God as confirming the moral prejudices that the audience already has. The thunder in *King Lear* is the tragically authentic voice of nature crumbling into chaos, though Lear himself half hopes that it is making a comment on his situation.

> —Northrop Frye, *Fools of Time: Studies in Shakespearean Tragedy* (Toronto: University of Toronto Press, 1967), pp. 115–16

❖

Roy W. Battenhouse on Lear's "Darker Purpose"

[Roy W. Battenhouse (b. 1912), formerly a professor of English at Indiana University, is the author of *Marlowe's* Tamburlaine: *A Study in Renaissance Moral Philosophy* (1941) and *A Companion to the Study of St. Augustine* (1955). In this extract, Battenhouse maintains that Lear's mention of a "darker purpose" reflects his own personal failings.]

Lear's opening words about a "darker purpose" carry a Shakespearean irony, since the purpose is here indeed darker than its speaker knows. He identifies his purpose as a publishing now of the dowries of his daughters in order that future strife may be prevented. The way in which he goes about this purpose, however, actually elicits strife—not only between the daughters as they are invited to compete in giving Lear adulation, but between himself and the favored daughter who fails to honor him to his liking. The incitements to strife lurk both in his imperiousness of manner (his commands to "Attend. . . .

Tell me. . . . Speak") and in the lush description he gives of the lands to be awarded. The very map of them so absorbs Lear's imagination that nothing is said of their magistracy, of the responsibility of ruling them. And then when his preferred child attempts a reply of impartial judgment, we see how superficial is his own imagined impartiality. Lear's actions thus publish to us his deeper purpose, an unacknowledged love of esteem which is at odds with his professed purpose of self-abnegation in resigning the throne.

Moreover, the self-abnegation itself is voiced in ominous phrasings. Lear says his "fast intent" is to "shake all cares." May this not mean a shaking off of all caring for human welfare? He speaks of desiring to be unburdened that he may "crawl toward death." Does not this suggest an unburdening of concern for life—and of his duty simply as a man to do something other than crawl? The Leir of Shakespeare's source play (dated about 1594) declared an intention to resort to "prayers and beades," whereby he might "thinke upon the welfare of my soule." Shakespeare's Lear uses no such language. He seems to be interested, rather, in his present opportunity for some *show* of self-abnegation by which to appear praiseworthy in the public eye. In dramatizing himself as one who will "crawl toward death," he is unaware that ironically he will be reduced to just such a crawl as the consequence of deluding himself regarding his real inner intentions.

Lear's purpose is dark enough to involve him in unwitting hypocrisy. He evades mentioning, until late in the scene, his intent to retain "the name and all the additions to a king." Furthermore, when he confesses that he had "thought to set my rest" on Cordelia's "kind nursery," he omits referring to the hundred knights he intended bringing into that nursery to serve him; mention of them is deferred until he can tuck in this detail subordinately to his granting of new largess to Goneril and Regan. What he gives must seem everything, and what he retains inconsequential. Yet Goneril will later describe Lear's retainers as making her castle "more like a tavern or a brothel / Than a graced palace." And allow as we may for exaggeration on Goneril's part, it nevertheless is clear that Lear's hidden purpose has been to buy by his "giving" a private preserve for self-indulgent living. Dramatically we have been shown contradictory "divesting." Lear has resigned the crown, but not with a desire to resign worldliness for humility. Instead his longing is for a superwordly status—essentially for the freedom of a demigod, accountable to no one outside himself.

—Roy W. Battenhouse, *Shakespearean Tragedy: Its Art and Its Christian Premises* (Bloomington: Indiana University Press, 1969), pp. 279–80

FRANK KERMODE ON DELUSIONS AND REALITY IN *KING LEAR*

[Frank Kermode (b. 1919), formerly the King Edward VII Professor of English at King's College, Cambridge, is one of the most distinguished literary critics of our time. Among his many works are *Shakespeare, Spenser, Donne* (1971), *English Renaissance Literature* (1974), and *An Appetite for Poetry* (1989). In this extract, Kermode comments on King Lear's two bodies, one natural and the other artificial.]

In this play, not for the first time, Shakespeare concerns himself with the contrast between the two bodies of the king: one lives by ceremony, administers justice in a furred gown, distinguished by regalia which set him above nature. The other is born naked, subject to disease and pain, and protected only by the artifices of ceremony from natural suffering and nakedness. So Lear is stripped, and moves from the ceremonies of the first scene to the company of the naked 'natural', the thing itself. The play deals with what intervenes between our natural and our artificially comfortable conditions: ceremony, justice, love, evil. Since our defenses against nature are fallible we need to learn the patience to do without them. On the heath any shelter is a grace, and there too the ceremonious folly of the Court Fool yields to the authentic natural madness of Poor Tom. Robbed by the contrivances which make life tolerable, we are like men at the end of the world, when no hope can exist except of an end and a divine judgement; but the pain, though terrible, is never at an end, the trial can be protracted beyond our worst imagining.

Lear does not *say* such things, it only presents them. It forces us to contemplate what, day in and day out, we prefer to forget: this is what it can be like, this is what it can mean to be human. Its characters jump, as we do, to their premature conclusions: Gloucester sees men as a game for the gods, but later he calls the gods 'ever gentle'; Albany sees the operation of justice in the death of Cornwall; Cordelia says the gods are 'kind'. As in life there are indications of providence, demands upon fortitude, occasions of despair. The end is woe and nakedness. But the play is not committed; it only shows us humanity at the cliff-edge of its own imaginings. It allows Lear his beautiful delusions of a life with Cordelia. It gives to the encounter of Lear and Gloucester at Dover, which I take to be the highest point in the history of tragedy, the blaze of human imagination, the full power of human speech. And however we may dwell upon the detail—the fashion of such themes as nature, clothing, nothingness, sight—we shall only possess the play by a living submission to it, and by a readiness to accept that each of us, in the course of a lifetime, may well—as if we too were a succession of different persons and different periods—know many different versions of *King Lear*.
—Frank Kermode, "Introduction," *Shakespeare:* King Lear: *A Casebook*, ed. Frank Kermode (London: Macmillan, 1969), pp. 20–21

❖

RUTH NEVO ON THE IMPORTANCE OF LOVE IN *KING LEAR*

[Ruth Nevo (b. 1924), formerly a professor of English at the University of Jerusalem, is the author of *Comic Transformations in Shakespeare* (1980) and *Shakespeare's Other Language* (1987). In this extract from *Tragic Form in Shakespeare* (1972), Nevo argues that love lies at the heart of *King Lear* and relates it to the Book of Job.]

The influence of Christian moral doctrine upon the interpretation of *King Lear* has given us the story of a penitent's progress through a school of suffering to the great spiritual discovery of love. One characteristic formulation is : ". . . the declining action which is the dogging of the hero to death is complemented by a rising action which is the hero's regeneration. . . . Its primary story is not the descent of the King into Hell but the ascent of the King as he climbs the mountain of Purgatory and is fulfilled." This view has been presented with varying degrees of subtlety, with varying degrees of allowance for the obdurate residue of pain and loss, with varying degrees of analytical sophistication. And indeed it has much to substantiate it. The highly symmetrical morality play grouping, suggesting Everyman traveling toward Death between false friends and true friends; the plenitude of references to the great topics of Christian reflection—*nosce teipsum* ⟨know thyself⟩, man and nature, providence, wisdom and folly, deceptive appearances; the powerful polarization of good and evil; the story of the Abasement of the Proud King: all lend themselves to assimilation in the direction of Christian myth, particularly if one is permitted to invoke what Enid Welsford has called "the wilder paradoxes" of the Christian religion. Yet the optimistic Christian reading fails to take adequate account of Lear's state of mind at the close of the play. It imposes upon what is exhibited the idea that Lear, having passed through the refining fires of affliction and attained humility, patience and self-knowledge, is thereby redeemed: "*King Lear* is, like the *Paradiso*, a vast poem on the victory of true love." ⟨R. W. Chambers⟩ Opponents of this view will be quick to point out that what we witness is considerably more in the nature of a defeat than a victory, that love proves to be the ultimate and most bitter mockery of the human condition, and that the unholy *pietà* of the final scene, as Lear enters with Cordelia in his arms, is an appalling parody not less than satanic in its import.

It is my purpose here to argue that love has only obliquely to do with the case, though filial reconciliation has seldom been more movingly portrayed; that it is the inadequacy, if anything, of love to redeem that is the burden of the play, though love is given, in Cordelia, France, the Fool, Kent, Gloucester, Edgar, in the obscure impulse which moves Cornwall's servants to turn against their master and succor a blind old man, and in Lear himself, a rich variety of forms more compelling, persuasive, and ethically appealing than in any other of the great tragedies; that what is enacted is a titanic agon rather than a purgatorial progress; and that the death of Cordelia, at which the sensibility of the eighteenth century shuddered, and which the sensibility of the twentieth century shudderingly embraces, is dramatically intelligible. By dramatically intelligible, I mean intelligible not in terms either of a providentialist or a nihilist philosophy, but in terms of that tragic movement of the spirit which the play dramatizes, a necessary part of the self-discovery of which the play is a mimesis.

The sins of Lear, for which, it is so often held, he is punished, have been indefatigably catalogued. Wicked pride, self-will, self-love, vanity, choler, egoism, senile puerility, a crass materialism which views love as a commodity to be bartered and traded, tyranny, sloth, and want of courage, which lays down burdens and offers as rationalization the excuse of old age—all have found their place, severally and together, in the indictment of Lear. And as the indictment grows heavier, the punishment becomes more and more deserved, at the very least justifiable upon Regan's pedagogic grounds:

> O! Sir, to willful men,
> The injuries that they themselves procure
> Must be their schoolmasters.   (II.iv.304–306)

The play makes Regan the spokesman of this cold self-righteousness, rendering further comment unnecessary. But under any guise, the moral sense which can be stilled by the logic of Job's comforters is probably impervious to tragic experience. Bildadism is so prevalent in the criticism of King Lear, I suggest, because the play is a Shakespearean version of the Book of Job, raising the problem of undeserved suffering with a similar insistence, power, and intensity. The Elizabethans saw Job as the pattern of all patience which Lear invokes on the heath; but in the rebellion which is a constitutive part of that ancient contest with God the imagination reared upon the Scriptures could hardly have failed to find the paradigm of what ⟨Alfred⟩ Harbage has so perceptively isolated for comment: "Lear's molten indignation, his huge invective, his capacity for feeling pain."

—Ruth Nevo, *Tragic Form in Shakespeare* (Princeton: Princeton University Press, 1972), pp. 258–61

❖

BERNARD MCELROY ON THE NATURE OF A MONARCH'S POWER

[Bernard McElroy (1938–1991), a former professor of English at Loyola University of Chicago, wrote *Fiction of the Modern Grotesque* (1989) and *Shakespeare's Mature Tragedies* (1973), from which the following extract is taken. Here, McElroy explores Shakespeare's fascination with the relationship between "the power and the powerlessness of the monarch."]

From the earliest days of his career, Shakespeare appears to have been fascinated by the problematic relationship between the power and powerlessness of the monarch, between the king's divine office and the king's mortality. Reflections upon that conflict constitute the only memorable speech of Henry VI; the insubstantiality of kingly power is Richard II's favorite subject and Henry IV's most unsettling worry; thoughts of his own frailty trouble even the redoubtable Harry the Fifth on the eve of his greatest triumph. Shakespeare renders his definitive treatment of the theme in *King Lear*. In the history plays, however, the struggle for power—its ins and outs, its changing fortunes, personalities, stratagems, machinations, and ultimate outcome—is of paramount interest. In *Lear,* on the other hand, the struggle becomes almost incidental to the real business of the tragedy: the crude wresting of power from the weak by the strong provides the context in which men of extraordinary passion and commitment confront the possibility, indeed the inescapability, of a violent, anarchic universe, wholly without a stable, inherent structure and utterly devoid of meaning. Faced with such a possibility, Lear is forced to ask himself and the cosmos a series of questions, the answers to which hold terrible implications. If the hierarchy of state and family is not real, then what is? If he is not the king, then who or what is he? If the bonds of nature are not sanctioned by divine ordination, than what holds the world together? If the trappings of civilization are superfluous "lendings," then what differentiates man from the animals? If the heavens are indifferent, if they do not love old men, if their sweet sway does not allow—*demand*— obedience, if they themselves are not old except in the myths of a collective imagination, if they do not send down and take the part of outraged kings and wronged fathers, then what becomes of justice and morality? If kingship itself is not a divinely established office, then what is the great image of authority?

More than any other of the mature tragedies, *King Lear* has conveyed the unmistakable impression of creating the unique universe in which it takes place. Critics as far removed from each other in time, technique, and point of view as A. C. Bradley, G. Wilson Knight, and Maynard Mack have all analyzed the universe of *Lear,* and terms such as "*Lear*-world" or its equivalents occur again and again in the work of dozens of commentators. Perhaps the reason for the ubiquitous feeling that the world of *King Lear* is self-created and self-defining is that life in that world is so far removed from literal experience not only of Shakespeare's England but also of any historical period which he might have thought he was recreating. In *Hamlet* and *Othello,* the dramatist relied heavily upon the conventions and trappings of life in Renaissance Europe, but, in *King Lear,* he seemed expressly to avoid transposing the old legend into contemporary times, in contrast to the author of the probable source play, *The True Chronicle History of King Leir.* Nor do I think he was attempting to recreate the atmosphere and life style of an ancient civilization, as he so manifestly was in the Roman plays. Rather, it seems to me, the setting of the *Lear*-world is an amalgam in which borrowings from several different eras and civilizations are fused for particular dramatic purposes, the two most important epochs being the Middle Ages and Shakespeare's own time. *King Lear* is, among many other things, a paradigm of the waning medieval hierarchy confronting the onset of pragmatic materialism. As John Danby has pointed out, it reflects Hooker while anticipating Hobbes.

In no play since *Richard II* did Shakespeare so conspicuously incorporate the forms, conventions, and ideas of medieval times. The most obvious examples are the pomp and pageantry of the distinctly feudal court in the first scene and the trial by combat in the last, both of which have close parallels in *Richard II*. Far more significant, however, is the inclusion of so many medieval attitudes and ideas, beginning with the idea of kingship itself. When he first appears, Lear is an openly absolute monarch of the kind England had not seen in centuries (if, in fact, it had ever seen one). Claudius, like his Tudor counterparts, had to submit his judgments to a privy council, being careful not to bar their better wisdoms, and the Duke of Venice, like the Stuarts, had a legislative body to deal with. But Lear's word, like Richard's, is absolute law, no matter how rash or foolish that word may be. To disobey, or even to disagree, is tantamount to treason and risks the gravest consequences. Hence there is no middle ground between acquiescence and usurpation, a fact as instrumental to Lear's tragedy as to Richard's.

—Bernard McElroy, *Shakespeare's Mature Tragedies* (Princeton: Princeton University Press, 1973), pp. 145–47

PAUL DELANY ON FEUDALISM AND *KING LEAR*

[Paul Delany (b. 1937), formerly a professor of English at Simon Fraser University (Burnaby, British Columbia), is the author of several critical works including *D. H. Lawrence's Nightmare* (1978) and *The Neo-Pagans: Rupert Brooke and the Ordeal of Youth* (1987). In this extract, Delany examines the political, social, and economic implications of *King Lear* and its historical setting.]

Shakespeare lived at a time when an uncertain balance had been struck in the transition from the feudal-aristocratic society of medieval England to the emergent bourgeois state. The aristocracy and the bourgeoisie were a rough match for each other in power, cohesion, and self-confidence; each had its characteristic moral values and style of life, and each claimed that its own way constituted "human nature": the personality typical of a particular class was elevated to a norm that all mankind should recognize. *King Lear* pits these rival concepts of human nature against each other in sharp and mutually explosive opposition. In such a conflict, one would expect Marx's sympathies to be given wholeheartedly to the historically progressive energies of the bourgeoisie; but his discussion of it in *The Communist Manifesto* is in fact strongly ambivalent:

> The bourgeoisie, wherever it has gotten the upper hand, has put an end to all feudal, patriarchal, idyllic relations. It has pitilessly torn asunder the motley feudal ties that bound man to his "natural superiors," and has left remaining no other nexus between man and man than naked self-interest, than callous "cash payment." It has drowned the most heavenly ecstasies of religious fervour, of chivalrous enthusiasm, of philistine sentimentalism, in the icy water of egotistical calculation. It has resolved personal worth into exchange value, and in place of the numberless indefeasible chartered freedoms, has set up that single, unconscionable freedom—Free Trade.

In this elegy for a dying culture Marx seems dismayed by the human costs of the breakup of the feudal order and appalled by the moral nihilism of those who destroyed it. Elsewhere, in more splenetic moods, he may delight in consigning some losing cause to the "rubbish heap of history"; but the achievement of feudalism he finds too appealing to be thus summarily dismissed. No matter how greedy, inefficient, and exploitive the feudal church and aristocracy may have been, their fervent idealism sustained man's sense of his own worth and of his right to his allotted place in the social hierarchy. The new order, however, having set up cash payment as the only measure of social obligation, ruthlessly attacks all customary bonds that impede the development of production and trade:

> Constant revolutionising of production, uninterrupted disturbance of all social conditions, everlasting uncertainty and agitation distinguish the bourgeois epoch from all earlier ones. All

fixed, fast-frozen relations, with their train of ancient and venerable prejudices and opinions, are swept away, all new-formed ones become antiquated before they can ossify. All that is solid melts into air, all that is holy is profaned, and man is at last compelled to face, with sober senses, his real conditions of life, and his relations with his kind.

In his appreciation of feudal values Marx revealed the chivalric idealism that still lingered from his adolescence and also, perhaps, his pride at having won the aristocrat Jenny von Westphal as his bride. His curiously nostalgic account of the decline of feudalism probably also reflects the influence of a man of kindred temperament, but opposite allegiance: Thomas Carlyle. *Past and Present* (1843) professes a devotion to the corporate society of medieval England and a horror of the moral vacuity of laissez-faire that are remarkably close in tone and diction to the analysis given five years later in *The Communist Manifesto:*

All this dire misery, therefore; all this of our poor Workhouse Workmen, of our Chartisms, Tradestrikes, Corn-Laws, Toryisms, and the general breakdown of Laissez-faire in these days,—may we not regard it as a voice from the dumb bosom of Nature, saying to us: Behold! Supply-and-demand is not the one Law of Nature; Cash-payment is not the sole nexus of man with man,— how far from it! Deep, far deeper than Supply-and-demand, are Laws, Obligations sacred as Man's Life itself: these also, if you will continue to do work, you shall now learn and obey.

In *King Lear* Shakespeare displays a similar attachment to traditional and aristocratic values, combined with a distaste and fear of the acquisitive, unscrupulous bourgeois values (as they appear to him) that are taking their place. His view of the classic conflict of his time is conditioned by that basic division in his temperament that is dramatized in his plays as the opposition of the Lion and the Fox. The Lion, or man of passion, Shakespeare usually represents as an aristocrat of the old style: noble, open, and generous, but flawed by his devotion to the formal ceremony and the quixotic gesture. His honorable simplicity ensures his defeat by the Fox, the cunning and ruthless devotee of Machiavellian *realpolitik.* In his history plays, Shakespeare inclines to a more skeptical view of the Lion's virtues. For the good of the kingdom, the rash and histrionic Lion must be supplanted by the politic Fox: thus Bolingbroke prevails over Richard, Hal over Hotspur. But in the tragedies the Lion's credulity is intrinsic to his noble nature, whereas the Fox's cunning is savage and nihilistic: Othello is overthrown by Iago, Lear and Gloucester by Regan, Goneril, and Edmund.

—Paul Delany, "*King Lear* and the Decline of Feudalism," *PMLA* 92, No. 3 (May 1977) : 429–31

William F. Zak on Cordelia

[William F. Zak is a professor of English at Salisbury State University in Salisbury, Maryland, and the author of *Sovereign Shame* (1984), a study of *King Lear* from which the following extract is taken. Here, Zak focuses on the character of Cordelia, who seems to represent a defiance of the play's dominant message of the meaninglessness of life.]

Though man is, by nature, a freakish creature who often deserves laughter—a featherless biped—he need not cripple his state further by hiding his defects or by brazening them out; he should, paradoxically, "cultivate" them and, thus, harmonize nature and merit. Cordelia and the Fool, though greatly pained by the miseries they see others experiencing, know, nonetheless, that is neither appropriate nor wise to be so ashamed of what is shameful in us that we fail to face ourselves and, consequently, live out a pretense of virtue, never honestly meeting each other or establishing true community. Gloucester may nearly boast to Kent of having overcome his shame for the bastard he engendered, but we know that he has neither faced his shame nor grown humbled by it. He has, instead, merely grown insensitive to it, compounding it rather than learning from it, nurturing Edmund's bastardy rather than Edmund himself. Both Gloucester and Edmund wrongly insist that their shame is barren when, in fact, it is the only soil in which their virtues can be cultivated. Similarly, Cordelia knows that Lear's shame is not an intolerable offense against the person he imagines he might otherwise have become; it is the very precondition of that character's possible flourishing. It is solely because Lear, Gloucester, Edmund, and Edgar cannot imagine so cultivating themselves that so much unnecessary devastation results.

But however torturing and grotesque the effects of their unwitting failure to face themselves, Cordelia's presence in the play also teaches us that our final response to them should not be judgment since in their hearts they are clearly more frightened than vicious, more threatened and unsure of themselves than selfish. Like her, we only wish that they might share a "better way" to cultivate shame than the pretense of shamelessness. Although man can be a contemptible animal, he is not irredeemably so. If this featherless creature cannot fly (the play is filled with the "images of revolt and flying off" [2.4.90]—all ultimately unsuccessful), he need not in self-contempt "top extremity" by cutting off his legs to spite his deformed wings and "crawl toward death," moving in self-pitying and self-condemning abdication from communality. For such logistical maneuvers are themselves as much a part of the revolt against acknowledgment of who we are and can be, as much a flight from self as their seeming opposite. Rather than fly or crawl we can, instead, with natural dignity, genuine merit, and the muted joy of fellowship stand together even when we "stand condemn'd" (1.4.5), as Cordelia, Kent, and the Fool reveal in their solidarity.

Man need not merely usurp his life; he can responsively live it, standing in each "instant" come what may, not fleeing the present as he orchestrates imperial designs upon his brave future. Such living, of course, is no easy accomplishment. In a sense, it is not an accomplishment at all but at best an abiding attitude of humility. Only through the dreadful insecurity involved in our truest acts of bravery, the continued submission of ourselves to the ever-changing demands of the moment and the people in them, ourselves included, and our untiring acknowledgments and admissions of our "mere defects" and failures, can we, like Cordelia under the tutelage of her shame, learn humility's difficult lesson, be "eas'd / With being nothing," and through that grow into the fully human stature of what Shelley called "self-empire and the majesty of love." In her natural slowness (France remarks upon the "tardiness" in her "nature" [1.1.235] not to censure but to praise her) Cordelia knows that the strange "art of our necessities . . . / [that] can make vild things precious" (3.2.70–71) is no alchemical quackery that can transform the security of our "means" from lead to gold instantaneously and at our impatient will, as Lear thinks it when he makes the statement; her slowness is, instead, a lifetime discipline, an art of living, that can gradually but miraculously transform the open and honest admission of our defects into emerging self-respect and the most shameful deformities of those we love into something precious. "Things base and vile, holding no quantity, / Love can transpose to form and dignity" (*Midsummer Night's Dream* 1.1.232–33). The reason such art is "strange" is not the inaccessibility of its mysteries but our refusal to become familiar with its practice. As Kent claims, Cordelia comes "seeking to give / Losses their remedies" (2.2.169–70); but few of us are willing to follow the dreadful cure of her homeopathy.

Cordelia is unquestionably the key to the play's sustaining vision. Readings that focus on Lear's redemption too conveniently tend to forget her death or trifle with it by denying its importance, as if they agreed with the logic that denies the importance of Cordelia's own life and happiness in Lear's "come, let's away to prison" speech. So-called absurdist readings, on the other hand, presumably following Gloucester's equally questionable accusation of the meaningless heavens, tend to forget the overwhelming meaningfulness of Cordelia alive in the play. Neither position adequately accounts for the subtlety of Cordelia and the Fool's vision and heroism, and both thus avoid a full recognition of the play's complexities. Cordelia and the Fool unobtrusively manifest the ideal tact, prudence, and engagement with life the others lack.

—William F. Zak, *Sovereign Shame: A Study of* King Lear (Lewisburg, PA: Bucknell University Press, 1984), pp. 55–57

C. L. BARBER AND RICHARD P. WHEELER ON LEAR'S SECOND CHILDHOOD

[C. L. Barber was a noted Shakespearean scholar who wrote *Shakespeare's Festive Comedy* (1959) and was working on *The Whole Journey* prior to his death in 1980. His colleague, Richard P. Wheeler (b. 1943), a professor of English at the University of Illinois, completed the work. In this extract, Barber and Wheeler relate Lear's madness to a return to a state of infancy.]

The play, in taking Lear into madness, takes him back to the source of the self in earliest infancy, to a deeper, more archaic level of being where self and world, child and parent, interpenetrate. With developments that accompany Lear's lapse into the madness he fears—"I prithee, daughter, do not make me mad" (II.iv.218)—the more general movement of the play unfolds as an experience of something like a world going mad. This is also the level of experience in which the need for the material, for the heritage of "basic trust" grounded in the earliest, cherishing bond to the mother, is substantive. Lear's need for it is expressed not only in his demand on his daughters, but also in his efforts to be or become the cherishing force he needs: by giving away the original inheritance (compare *Timon of Athens*), which makes him into a "sheal'd peascod"; by his solicitous regard for "my Boy," his Fool; by the generous wave of feeling he finds in himself in thinking about the "poor naked wretches" and Poor Tom; and finally by his eagerness, at the end, to give himself entirely to Cordelia, though he cannot see the destructive taking that is inseparable from this giving.

In his recognition of "unaccomodated man" in the guise of Poor Tom, in his savage railing at Dover—against "the sulphurous pit" of female sexuality, or against the "great image of authority: a dog's obey'd in office"—Lear envisages a universe stripped entirely of the kind of cherishing love that has its roots in the nurturant and nurturing experience shared by child and parent. But throughout his agonized repudiation of a world of savagery and corruption he remains the object of sympathetic, cherishing loyalty expressed by the Fool, Kent, Gloucester, Edgar, Albany, and others. Lear can hold the affection of so many characters, and of his audience, because he is parental as well as childlike, embodying the impossible but loving parent who is forgiven and affiliated to—as Kent affiliates, after saying that he can get along without Lear, just as Lear has said that he can get along without Cordelia. It is because he has so much sense of self (however shattered by developments that he puts in motion), and with it so much self to give, for others who have anchored their own identities in his royal presence, that he can command the reverential compassion of those for whom his madness is "a sight most pitiful in the meanest wretch, / Past speaking of in a king" (IV.vi.204–5). There is a fuller love expressed *for* Lear than for any other Shakespearean character. ⟨. . .⟩

How fully Shakespeare understood the destructive side of human bonds, the value of which he so movingly expresses, is manifest in his having changed the happy ending of all his sources. The English win, and among the English, Edmund. Lear's great speech in response to that situation is often quoted by those who, caught up in the Christian feeling, want to see the play's ending as wholly redemptive, with intimations of a reunion of father and daughter in a hereafter:

> Come, let's away to prison: . . .
> When thou dost ask me blessing, I'll kneel down
> And ask of thee forgiveness. So we'll live,
> And pray, and sing, and tell old tales, . . .
> And take upon 's the mystery of things
> As if we were God's spies.   (V.iii.8, 10–12, 16–17)

Lear has undergone a discipline of humility and achieved something like Christian disillusion with worldly things, together with a sense of the wrong he did Cordelia. He has seen through royal vanity. But he still wants his daughter "to love [her] father all." His vision of prison amounts, almost literally, to a conception of heaven on earth—*his* heaven, the "kind nursery" after all. A chasm of irony opens as we realize that he is leading her off to death. "Upon such sacrifices, my Cordelia, / The gods themselves throw incense" (V.iii.20–21). It is *her* sacrifice that the generous-hearted, loving old father is praising—the sacrifice she is to make, voluntarily, led on by love, but a sacrifice, finally, to his need for her. It is *her* sacrifice, made instead of the sacrifice that he in the first place refused, in refusing her dower, in refusing to give her away, in the deep sense outwardly symbolized by the marriage service.

To talk about what Shakespeare is appealing to (and controlling) in such a moment, one needs to understand the religious traditions or situation he is drawing on, and also the roots of potential religious feeling in the family. For the whole action of the play renews the springs of religious feeling, but without supernatural objects. He is presenting the modern situation where religious need, or need cognate to what has been dealt with by worship of the Holy Family, has no resource except the human family and its extensions in society, including the problematic ideal of kingship. William Elton's King Lear *and the Gods* shows how highly relevant the religious thought of the period is to the play—notably the idea of a *deus absconditus* ⟨the hidden god⟩. The play's adumbration of religious ritual is exhibited by Herbert Coursen's fine study entitled *Christian Ritual and the World of Shakespeare's Tragedies.* For my purposes, psychoanalysis is a useful supplement because it amounts, in some aspects, to a sociology of love and worship within the family, or derived from the family, especially as experienced in infancy.

The experiences of infancy were not, as such, a focus of much analytical attention in Shakespeare's period; our acute consciousness of them goes back to romanticism and develops along with the decreasing hold of religion. Infantile experience as such is also not a major concern of Shakespeare's art, since his culture little regarded it, except in displaced forms. Yet his plays find equivalents and shape action in ways that, with their central familial preoccupations, can be understood by reference to infantile residues. Thus it is useful, I think, to understand Lear's vision of prison as a regressive wish demanding that Cordelia join in it. In the large design of the play, this tendency connects with the childishness and playfulness, often charming and liberating in the midst of anguish, that floods through the Fool's part and flashes in moments in Edgar's impersonation of Mad Tom, as in Lear's own sprightliness in madness. The tendency also relates to Lear's confident assumption at the outset of relationship to a benign Nature, even as he asks the "dear goddess" to convey sterility into the womb of Goneril—with the developing ambiguities: Edmund's "lusty stealth of nature" (I.ii.11), Lear's incredulous "Is there any cause in nature that make these hard hearts?" (III.vi.77–78)

> —C. L. Barber and Richard P. Wheeler, *The Whole Journey: Shakespeare's Power of Development* (Berkeley: University of California Press, 1986), pp. 291–95

❖

ALEXANDER LEGGATT ON STAGING *KING LEAR*

[Alexander Leggatt (b. 1940), a professor of English at the University of Toronto, is the author of *Citizen Comedy in the Age of Shakespeare* (1973) and *Shakespeare's Political Drama: The History Plays and the Roman Plays* (1988). In this extract from his study of *King Lear* (1991), Leggatt examines the problems of staging the storm scene in the play.]

Among the play's staging problems the most notorious is the storm. In his prologue to *Every Man in His Humour* Ben Jonson pours a neoclassicist's scorn on the simple methods that were evidently used in Shakespeare's theatre; his list of promises about what his audience will *not* be subjected to includes

> nor roll'd bullet heard
> To say, it thunders, nor tempestuous drum
> Rumbles, to tell you when the storm doth come . . .

The nineteenth century, the great age of scenic elaboration, had the resources for a full-scale storm; but reviewers of Charles Kean's production complained that the shifting lights, rustling leaves (the threads that operated them were unfortunately visible) and general hubbub were distractions that drowned out the efforts of the actors. *The Times* concluded, 'He should have recollected that it is the bending of Lear's mind under his wrongs that is the object of interest, and not that of a forest beneath the hurricane. The machinery may be transferred to the next new pantomime.' The dangers of a 'realistic' storm whose fakery will at some point be obvious, and whose principal effect will be to drown out the actors, are plain enough. Yet in toning down the storm to something he could cope with Macready incurred the criticism that the effect was tame, and the grandeur of the scene was replaced by mere distress. The responsibility for the scene's effect is shared by the technicians and the leading actor. John Gielgud wrote of his 1931 performance, 'I was wholly inadequate in the storm scenes, having neither the voice nor the physique for them. Lear has to *be* the storm, but I could do no more than shout against the thundersheet.' Gielgud's view that Lear himself has to be the storm has been widely echoed; but it is a rare production that puts all the weight on the actor. This was tried in Glen Byam Shaw's 1959 production with Charles Laughton: there were visual effects of rain and cloud, but (accounts vary, and there seem to have been changes during the run) either no sound at all, or only minimal thunder and 'a distant hiss of rain' (*Daily Mail*, 19 August 1959). The experiment, like everything else about the production, divided the house; some appreciated the chance to listen to the speeches, others found the impact of the scene diminished. Peter Brook put his finger on the problem: 'there is a conflict. An actor can't make the energy and the dynamics of the storm scene any more than you can make a sculpture on water. It's like shadow-boxing. So there has to be an element that says "storm." ' The dialogue between Lear and the storm needs to be just that—a dialogue; not a competition in decibel levels. The answer finally lies not in the technology, which can be anything from a beaten drum to a Moog synthesiser, but in the intelligence with which the technology is used.

If the storm is the obvious problem of the play, there are other peculiarities that have to be coped with, that demand choices. The battle is the most perfunctory in Shakespeare. It is represented only by offstage sound, and the fact that Gloucester is on stage throughout implies that Shakespeare wanted the sound-battle to be brief. At the opposite extreme lies Akiro Kurosawa's film *Ran,* inspired by *King Lear,* which is full of spectacular images of war, images that seem for much of the film to be the principal vehicle for its vision of chaos. In our war-obsessed age there is always a temptation to do more with the battle than Shakespeare asks for; it is for us an inevitable image of cruelty and violence. In the Byam Shaw production, generally praised for its visual simplicity, primitive war-machines were dragged on stage and fired arrows into the wings. More recently, directors have gone in the direction of stylization: in Trevor Nunn's 1968 Royal Shakespeare Company production the battle was a slow-motion ballet freezing occasionally into tableaux, with Gloucester sitting in front, his head thrown back in a silent scream. Like the storm, the battle is a test of how far, and to what purpose, a production is prepared to elaborate on the text.

In the text itself the most appalling image of violence is not the battle but the blinding of Gloucester. Here the test is different: what will the production expect an audience to take? Recently, audiences have been made to face the full horror of it. But throughout the eighteenth and nineteenth centuries the scene was partially or entirely cut. When it was restored in the twentieth century, audiences found it hard to take. Hallam Fordham reported of the scene in Granville Barker's 1940 production, 'the effect was sufficient to cause some (and especially men!) to grope towards the exits with unbecoming haste.' In 1950 at Stratford-upon-Avon 'a few people had to be taken to the first aid department' (*Western Daily Press,* 21 July 1950). At the Old Vic between the wars, Lilian Baylis insisted that the blinding of Gloucester should come immediately after the interval, so that audience members who weren't up to it could wait it out in the lobby. This custom was observed in the Gielgud productions of 1940 and 1950. Byam Shaw in 1959 and Peter Brook in 1962 shifted the interval to just *after* the blinding of Gloucester, thus making the atrocity the climactic event of Act I. This decision about the interval, no less than the return of the full text, shows a change from a theatre that was prepared to spare its audience the more painful aspects of a play to a theatre that insisted on them—and a corresponding shift in the reading of the play itself.

—Alexander Leggatt, *King Lear* (Manchester: Manchester University Press, 1991), pp. 7–9

DAVID M. BERGERON ON LETTERS IN *KING LEAR*

[David M. Bergeron (b. 1938) is a professor of English at the University of Kansas. He has written *Shakespeare: A Study and Research Guide* (1975) and *Shakespeare's Romances and the Royal Family* (1985). In this extract, Bergeron studies letters in *King Lear* as a form of mediated discourse, creating common ground for both kings and writers.]

At the beginning of this century A. C. Bradley published his influential *Shakespearean Tragedy* where in the discussion of *Lear*, he aptly notes a series of "improbabilities" in the play. He writes: "The improbabilities in *King Lear* surely far surpass those of the other great tragedies in number and grossness. And they are particularly noticeable in the secondary plot. For example, no sort of reason is given why Edgar, who lives in the same house with Edmund, should write a letter to him instead of speaking; and this is a letter absolutely damning to his character." Only for a fleeting moment should this letter writing seem an improbability; numerous historical examples abound that reveal such correspondence between members of the same household. But I do not want to argue from historical evidence. Rather I will be maintaining that Shakespeare has placed an extraordinary reliance on letters in the Gloucester story in order to open up another level of discourse, one in contrast to Lear's. I will reflect on and expand some ideas from a brilliant essay by Sigurd Burckhardt, first published now thirty years ago.

Difficult to count precisely, numerous letters circulate in the play. Checking the Shakespeare concordance, I note that Shakespeare uses the word *letter* thirty-three times in *Lear*. No other tragedy comes close in such frequency. Interestingly, the use of *letter* corresponds exactly with the frequency of the word *nothing*, which also appears thirty-three times. I will resist for the moment the attempt to make something out of nothing. At the very least, however, we must in studying and thinking about this play pay attention to the quality of *nothing* and the *letter*. Commenting on the second scene of the play—the encounter between Gloucester and Edmund—Burckhardt writes: "With this scene, the letter becomes the emblem of the illicit and dangerously mediate—so clearly so that the sight of Lear reading a letter would strike us somehow incongruous; for a letter is speech reduced to signs, discourse become manifestly indirect." That is, a letter can only offer indirect, mediated discourse—signs, not reality. It exists on the paradoxical boundary between confrontation and report; in and of itself, for example, it offers no possibility of immediate correction, should it be misunderstood. It is; and we must make the best of it, reading between its lines in order to grasp the tone. By its indirection we attempt to find direction out.

Although Burkhardt says that the sight of Lear reading a letter would seem incongruous, I offer a slight modification by looking at a major source of Shakespeare's play, the anonymous play *King Leir,* dating from about 1594 and first published in 1605—not long before Shakespeare's version of the story. In the important scene 19 of the anonymous *Leir,* Leir and his companion Perillus, wandering through the countryside, pause to rest their weary bodies. They are sleepy; but Leir says: "Ile sit me downe, and read until she [a daughter] come." Apparently they have brought books with them. He later in that scene reads the letter from Gonorill that the Messenger has brought; it orders the murder of Leir. Mercifully, Leir and Perillus escape, thanks to the intervention of nature—much kinder in this play than in Shakespeare's—and the softening of the Messenger's heart. Shakespeare changes all of this and discharges such energy of reading principally in the Gloucester plot. To assist the comprehension that the letters may seem deadly, I will begin with the play's first scene in order to establish the context for letters as an alternative to Lear's pattern of discourse; I will draw on the anonymous *Leir.*

Shakespeare's play starts not with Lear but with Gloucester, who in the first 30 lines (or more precisely 33!) reveals to Kent the bastardy of his son Edmund, who accompanies him. In this amiable and non-threatening conversation Gloucester's acknowledgment of Edmund as his son strikes us as commendable, if unusual. And yet this somewhat peculiar manner in which to begin a drama presumably about Lear signals right away that Gloucester and the relationship to his sons may be important. It also opens this initial scene to at least four major violations of well-established principles: social, political, moral, and personal/familial. Gloucester has abrogated social custom and moral law by fathering an illegitimate son; Lear will rupture political convention by dividing the kingdom, and he will sever personal and familial bonds by the imposition of the love test. ⟨ . . .⟩

Shakespeare has sent us a letter: his mediated discourse of this play brings us nevertheless face to face with a direct awareness of suffering and leaves us struggling to answer some of life's hardest and harshest questions. Like Cordelia, we may simply utter "nothing" because language itself often remains inadequate to convey our feelings. The rest is silence.

—David M. Bergeron, "Deadly Letters in *King Lear*," *Philological Quarterly* 72, No. 2 (Spring 1993): 159–61, 174–75

❖

Works by
William Shakespeare

Venus and Adonis. 1593.

The Rape of Lucrece. 1594.

Henry VI. 1594.

Titus Andronicus. 1594.

The Taming of the Shrew. 1594.

Romeo and Juliet. 1597.

Richard III. 1597.

Richard II. 1597.

Love's Labour's Lost. 1598.

Henry IV. 1598.

The Passionate Pilgrim. 1599.

A Midsummer Night's Dream. 1600.

The Merchant of Venice. 1600.

Much Ado about Nothing. 1600.

Henry V. 1600.

The Phoenix and the Turtle. 1601.

The Merry Wives of Windsor. 1602.

Hamlet. 1603.

King Lear. 1608.

Troilus and Cressida. 1609.

Sonnets. 1609.

Pericles. 1609.

Othello. 1622.

Mr. William Shakespeares Comedies, Histories & Tragedies. Ed.
John Heminge and Henry Condell. 1623 (First Folio), 1632
(Second Folio), 1663 (Third Folio), 1685 (Fourth Folio).

Poems. 1640.

Works. Ed. Nicholas Rowe. 1709. 6 vols.

Works. Ed. Alexander Pope. 1723–25. 6 vols.

Works. Ed. Lewis Theobald. 1733. 7 vols.

Works. Ed. Thomas Hanmer. 1743–44. 6 vols.

Works. Ed. William Warburton. 1747. 8 vols.

Plays. Ed. Samuel Johnson. 1765. 8 vols.

Plays and Poems. Ed. Edmond Malone. 1790. 10 vols.

The Family Shakespeare. Ed. Thomas Bowdler. 1807. 4 vols.

Works. Ed. J. Payne Collier. 1842–44. 8 vols.

Works. Ed. H. N. Hudson. 1851–56. 11 vols.

Works. Ed. Alexander Dyce. 1857. 6 vols.

Works. Ed. Richard Grant White. 1857–66. 12 vols.

Works (Cambridge Edition). Ed. William George Clark, John
Glover, and William Aldis Wright. 1863–66. 9 vols.

A New Variorum Edition of the Works of Shakespeare.
Ed. H. H. Furness et al. 1871– .

Works. Ed. W. J. Rolfe. 1871–96. 40 vols.

The Pitt Press Shakespeare. Ed. A. W. Verity. 1890–1905.
13 vols.

The Warwick Shakespeare. 1893–1938. 13 vols.

The Temple Shakespeare. Ed. Israel Gollancz. 1894–97. 40 vols.

The Arden Shakespeare. Ed. W. J. Craig, R. H. Case et al.
1899–1924. 37 vols.

The Shakespeare Apocrypha. Ed. C. F. Tucker Brooke. 1908.

The Yale Shakespeare. Ed. Wilbur L. Cross, Tucker Brooke, and Willard Highley Durham. 1917–27. 40 vols.

The New Shakespeare (Cambridge Edition). Ed. Arthur Quiller-Couch and John Dover Wilson. 1921–62. 38 vols.

The New Temple Shakespeare. Ed. M. R. Ridley. 1934–36. 39 vols.

Works. Ed. George Lyman Kittredge. 1936.

The Penguin Shakespeare. Ed. G. B. Harrison. 1937–59. 36 vols.

The New Clarendon Shakespeare. Ed. R. E. C. Houghton. 1938– .

The Arden Shakespeare. Ed. Una Ellis-Fermor et al. 1951– .

The Complete Pelican Shakespeare. Ed. Alfred Harbage. 1969.

The Complete Signet Classic Shakespeare. Ed. Sylvan Barnet. 1972.

The Oxford Shakespeare. Ed. Stanley Wells. 1982– .

The New Cambridge Shakespeare. Ed. Philip Brockbank. 1984– .

Works about William Shakespeare and King Lear

Anderson, Judith H. "The Conspiracy of Realism: Impasse and Vision in *King Lear." Studies in Philology* 84 (1987): 1–23.

Bayley, John. *Shakespeare and Tragedy.* London: Routledge & Kegan Paul, 1981, pp. 7–48.

Bloom, Harold, ed. *William Shakespeare's* King Lear. New York: Chelsea House, 1987.

Booth, Stephen. King Lear, Macbeth, *Indefinition, and Tragedy.* New Haven: Yale University Press, 1983.

Brockbank, Philip. " 'Upon Such Sacrifices.' " *Proceedings of the British Academy* 62 (1976): 109–34.

Brownlow, F. W. *Shakespeare, Harsnett, and the Devils of Denham.* Newark: University of Delaware Press, 1993.

Burke, Kenneth. "*King Lear:* Its Form and Psychosis." *Shenandoah* 21 (1969–70): 3–19.

Calderwood, James L. "Creative Uncreation in *King Lear." Shakespeare Quarterly* 37 (1986): 5–19.

Cavell, Stanley. "The Avoidance of Love: A Reading of *King Lear.*" In Cavell's *Must We Mean What We Say?* New York: Scribner's, 1969, pp. 267–353.

Champion, Larry S. *Shakespeare's Tragic Perspective.* Athens: University of Georgia Press, 1976.

Colie, Rosalie L., and F. T. Flahiff, ed. *Some Facets of* King Lear: *Essays in Prismatic Criticism.* Toronto: University of Toronto Press, 1974.

Creeth, Edmund. "The King of Life in *King Lear.*" In Creeth's *Mankynde in Shakespeare.* Athens: University of Georgia Press, 1976, pp. 111–51.

Critical Survey 3, No. 3 (1991). Special *King Lear* issue.

Danby, John F. *Shakespeare's Doctrine of Nature: a Study of* King Lear. London: Faber & Faber, 1949.

Danson, Lawrence. *Tragic Alphabet: Shakespeare's Drama of Language.* New Haven: Yale University Press, 1974.

Elton, William R. King Lear *and the Gods.* San Marino, CA: Huntington Library, 1966.

Erickson, Peter. *Patriarchal Structures in Shakespeare's Drama.* Berkeley: University of California Press, 1985.

Everett, Barbara. "The New King Lear." *Critical Quarterly* 2 (1960): 325–39.

Foakes, R. A. Hamlet *versus* Lear: *Cultural Politics and Shakespeare's Art.* Cambridge: Cambridge University Press, 1993.

Foreman, Walter C., Jr. *The Music of the Close: The Final Scenes of Shakespeare's Tragedies.* Lexington: University Press of Kentucky, 1978.

Fraser, Russell A. *Shakespeare's Politics in Relation to* King Lear. London: Routledge & Kegan Paul, 1962.

Goldberg, S. L. *An Essay on* King Lear. Cambridge: Cambridge University Press, 1974.

Graham, Kenneth J. E. " 'Without the Form of Justice': Plainness and the Performance of Love in *King Lear.*" *Shakespeare Quarterly* 42 (1991): 438–61.

House, Ian W. O. " 'I Know Thee Well Enough': The Two Plots of *King Lear.*" *English* No. 170 (Summer 1992): 97–112.

Jorgensen, Paul A. *Lear's Self-Discovery.* Berkeley: University of California Press, 1967.

Kallendorf, Craig. "*King Lear* and the Figures of Speech." *Explorations in Renaissance Culture* 18 (1992): 1–25.

Kirsch, Arthur. "The Emotional Landscape of *King Lear.*" *Shakespeare Quarterly* 39 (1988): 154–70.

Leggatt, Alexander. *King Lear.* Boston: Twayne, 1988.

Lothian, John M. King Lear: *A Tragic Reading of Life.* Toronto: Clark, Irwin, 1949.

Mack, Maynard, Jr. King Lear *in Our Time*. Berkeley: University of California Press, 1965.

Martin, William F. *The Indissoluble Knot: King Lear as Ironic Drama*. Lanham, MD: University Press of America, 1987.

Mason, H. A. *Shakespeare's Tragedy of Love*. London: Chatto & Windus, 1970.

Murphy, John L. *Darkness and Devils: Exorcism and* King Lear. Athens: Ohio University Press, 1984.

Oates, Joyce Carol. " 'Is This the Promised End?' The Tragedy of *King Lear*." In Oates's *Contraries*. New York: Oxford University Press, 1981, pp. 51–81.

Reibetanz, John. *The* Lear *World: A Study of* King Lear *in Its Dramatic Context*. Toronto: University of Toronto Press, 1977.

Rosenberg, Marvin. *The Masks of* King Lear. Berkeley: University of California Press, 1972.

Schell, Edgar. *Strangers and Pilgrims: From* The Castle of Perseverance *to* King Lear. Chicago: University of Chicago Press, 1983.

Selden, Raman. "*King Lear* and True Need." *Shakespeare Studies* 19 (1987): 143–70.

Shakespeare Survey 13 (1960). Special *King Lear* issue.

Shakespeare Survey 33 (1980). Special *King Lear* issue.

Snyder, Susan. "Between the Divine and the Absurd: *King Lear*." In Snyder's *The Comic Matrix of Shakespeare's Tragedies*. Princeton: Princeton University Press, 1979, pp. 137–79.

Whitaker, Virgil K. *The Mirror Up to Nature: The Technique of Shakespeare's Tragedies*. San Marino, CA: Huntington Library, 1965.

Whitehead, Frank. "The Gods in *King Lear*." *Essays in Criticism* 42 (1992): 196–220.

Winstanley, Lilian. Macbeth, King Lear, *and Contemporary History*. Cambridge: Cambridge University Press, 1922.

Wittreich, Joseph. *"Image of That Horror": History, Prophecy, and Apocalypse in* King Lear. San Marino, CA: Huntington Library, 1984.

Index of
Themes and Ideas

ALBANY, DUKE OF, and his role in the play, 13, 15, 16, 18, 20, 21–22, 24, 25, 26, 27, 33, 43, 47, 53, 58, 69

AS YOU LIKE IT, as it compares, 33

CORDELIA, and her role in the play, 13, 14, 15, 19, 22, 23, 24, 25, 26, 27, 28, 30, 31, 33, 35, 36, 37, 38, 39, 41, 42, 43, 44, 47, 51, 53, 54, 55, 56, 58, 59, 60, 66–68, 69, 70, 71, 77

CORNWALL, DUKE OF, and his role in the play, 13, 16, 17, 18, 19, 20, 22, 23, 24, 27, 28, 43, 47, 53, 58

DIVINE COMEDY, THE (Dante), as it compares, 54, 59

EDGAR, and his role in the play, 14, 15, 16, 17, 20, 21, 23, 24, 25, 26, 27, 28, 35, 36, 43, 47, 50, 57, 60, 67, 69, 71, 75

EDMUND, and his role in the play, 13, 14, 15, 16, 17, 19, 20, 21, 22, 23, 24, 25, 26, 28, 30, 31–33, 35, 36, 42, 47, 66, 67, 70, 72, 75, 76

FOOL, THE, and his role in the play, 16, 17, 20, 28, 36, 50, 51, 60, 66, 67, 68, 69

GLOUCESTER, EARL OF, and his role in the play, 13, 14, 16,17, 19, 20, 21, 22, 23, 24, 25, 27, 28, 30, 32, 36, 43, 44, 45, 46, 47, 49, 50, 58, 60, 66, 67, 68, 69, 74, 75, 76, 77

GONERIL, and her role in the play, 13, 15, 16, 17, 18, 20, 21, 22, 24, 25, 27, 28, 35, 36, 40, 42, 47, 48, 50, 53, 55, 56, 66, 71, 76

HAMLET, as it compares, 36, 45, 51, 62

JUSTICE, as theme, 19, 20, 21, 23, 31, 38, 41, 45, 58

KENT, EARL OF, and his role in the play, 13, 15, 16, 17, 18, 19, 22, 24, 25, 26, 28, 36, 38, 39, 42, 43, 44, 47, 49, 50, 60, 66, 67, 68, 69, 70, 76

KING LEAR: and age in, 41–43; delusions and reality in, 57–58; and evil in, 46–48; failings of, 35–37; and feudalism, 63–66; and letters in, 75–77; the importance of love in, 58–61; and the nature of a monarch's power, 52–53, 61–63; and moral issues in, 29–31; the pessimism of, 33–35; and regeneration in, 44–46; the staging of, 72–74; thematic and structural analysis of, 13–26; tragedy and melodrama in, 54–55

LEAR: and the nature of kingship, 52–53, 61–63; and his madness, 48–51; and his role in the play, 13, 14, 16, 17, 18, 19, 20, 21, 22, 23, 24, 25, 26, 27, 28, 29, 33, 34, 35, 36, 42, 43, 44, 45, 46, 47, 55, 56, 57, 58, 59, 60, 66, 67, 68, 73, 75, 76, 77; and his second childhood, 69–72; and Tolstoy and renunciation, 39–41; the vanity of, 37–39

MACBETH, as it compares, 40, 46, 51

NATURAL ORDER, THE, as theme, 14, 16, 18, 23, 42–43, 44, 45, 46, 48, 52, 55, 76

OLIVER *(AS YOU LIKE IT),* as compared to Edmund, 33

OPHELIA *(HAMLET),* as compared to Lear, 36

OSWALD, and his role in the play, 15, 16, 17, 18, 20, 21, 22, 23, 24, 28

OTHELLO, as it compares, 40, 45, 62

REGAN, and her role in the play, 13, 15, 16, 17, 18, 19, 20, 21, 22, 24, 25, 27, 28, 35, 36, 40, 42, 43, 47, 53, 55, 56, 60, 66

RENUNCIATION, as theme, 39–41

RICHARD II, as it compares, 61, 63

SHAKESPEARE, WILLIAM, life of, 8–12

SIGHT, as theme, 13, 15, 21, 24, 27, 30, 34, 69

TIMON *(Timon of Athens),* as compared to Lear, 34, 69

TIMON OF ATHENS, as it compares, 34, 40, 69

TOLSTOY, LEO, and *King Lear,* 35–38, 39–41

TOM. *See* EDGAR

TRUE CHRONICLE HISTORY OF KING LEIR, as it compares, 56, 62, 76